Fun Facts Of Stupendous Stories Of Royal Love

Extraordinary Ruptures, Dramatic Divorces, and Unimaginable Scandals in Royal Relationships from Global Monarchies Across Centuries, with Interpretation and Marriage Lessons.

NICCI BROCHARD
&
DR. BEN CHUBA

Fun Facts Of Stupendous Stories Of Royal Love

Extraordinary Ruptures, Dramatic Divorces, and Unimaginable Scandals in Royal Relationships from Global Monarchies Across Centuries, with Interpretation and Marriage Lessons.

Book Formatting by: *Accuracy4sure*

Book cover design by: *MoNish*

CROSSBORDER

New York, London, Quebec

Contents

Chapter 11: Lessons from the Crown – Interpreting Love, Power, and Legacy

Epilogue: The Final Curtain on Crowned Capers

Prologue

Who needs reality TV when you have actual royalty? For centuries, kings and queens across the globe have been dishing out drama more lavish than their crown jewels and spicier than the gossip at a medieval banquet. Welcome to a world where royal romance goes delightfully wrong, where the stakes are high (empires have literally hung in the balance over a lover's spat) and the antics are outrageously human.

You'll sneak a peek at torrid love triangles in Versailles – imagine a king, a queen, and a royal mistress in a pas de trois that could give any soap opera a run for its money. You'll witness a full-blown royal hissy fit over something as trivial as breakfast toast (why not upend a kingdom over an overcooked slice of bread?). And yes, there's even an emperor who ghosted his empress by fleeing across continents, in what might be history's most literal case of "it's not you, it's me – I just have to rule over there... bye!"

No crown was sturdy enough to keep a royal heart in check. One English monarch took "till death do us part" a tad too literally (his breakup strategy involved a headsman and a whole new church). Another king abdicated the throne to marry his scandalous sweetheart (a questionable career move, but love makes us do silly things). Meanwhile, somewhere in a sultan's palace, a hundred concubines roll their eyes as a lovelorn ruler insists *this* time he's really found "The One."

As we romp through these tales of passion, power, and public peccadilloes, one thing becomes clear: beneath all the ermine and etiquette, royals are as ridiculously human as the rest of us when Cupid's arrow misfires. And yet, for all the absurdity, this cavalcade of royal misadventures will entertain as much as it enlightens. Sure, you're here for the scandals and giggles (and you'll get plenty), but don't be surprised if you also glean surprisingly useful relationship wisdom from history's most ostentatious romantic messes. After all, if a king's petty quarrel can spark a civil war, maybe we can learn to say "sorry" before someone feels the urge to call in the cavalry. So, tighten your tiara, dear reader, and prepare for a royally good time – with a wink, a nudge, and maybe a marriage lesson or two served alongside the scandals.

Ben and myself (Nicci), wish you a scintillating read. Thank you in advance for choosing our book.

Chapter 1

The Power of Passion—
Forbidden Love and the Price of Desire

Imagine a royal love so intense it topples a dynasty, builds a wonder of the world, or upends a kingdom's protocol. History is full of these "you can't make this up" romances. In this chapter, we travel from ancient Egypt to imperial India to modern Britain, uncovering how forbidden love affairs ignited political firestorms. It's a journey through grand passion and even grander consequences. And yes, we'll sprinkle in a bit of wit and modern flair—because if you think today's tabloids are wild, wait until you hear what *Cleopatra, Shah Jahan,* and *King Edward VIII* got up to.

These stories show that when love and duty clash, the fallout can be downright imperial, and the allure of transgression can prove irresistible. Buckle up for a narrative tour of three iconic romances that prove the heart wants what it wants even if it sends empires spinning.

Cleopatra, Julius Caesar and Mark Antony: Love Amidst Empires (Egypt & Rome)

Cleopatra VII of Egypt knew a thing or two about drama. As the last pharaoh of the Ptolemaic line, she inherited a kingdom in turmoil and a rendezvous with destiny. How to secure her throne against rivals and Roman interference? According to legend, the young queen literally *unrolled* the red carpet for love. One evening in 48 BC, Julius Caesar—Rome's most powerful man—was in Alexandria, likely not expecting a surprise package. Suddenly, a rug unfurled at his feet and out tumbled 21-year-old Cleopatra, daring, charismatic, and ready to beguile the 52-year-old general. It was an entrance so bold and cinematic that even Hollywood couldn't resist.

This was no mere fling in Caesar's eyes, he was enthralled. Cleopatra had intellect and charm by the bucketload (more *girlboss* than seductress stereotype), and Caesar was smitten enough to ignore the obvious: he had a wife back in Rome. The affair caused tongues to wag from the Nile to the Tiber. Caesar installed Cleopatra as co-ruler of Egypt almost immediately, solidifying her power.

Soon Cleopatra bore him a son (nicknamed *Caesarion*), and in a move that today would break the internet, she actually visited Rome as Caesar's *unofficial* guest. Picture the scene: Cleopatra arrives in Rome with exotic style, hosting lavish parties and getting a golden statue of herself erected in Caesar's temple. Romans were scandalized—here was their dictator-for-life flaunting a foreign queen in the capital, and a married foreign queen at that (the audacity!). It was as if the Emperor of Rome had brought a celebrity girlfriend home, and conservative Roman society collectively clutched its pearls. Cleopatra, however, was the star of the show, and Caesar didn't care who knew it.

Alas, their politically charged romance was cut short by daggers. When Julius Caesar was assassinated in 44 BC, Cleopatra had to flee Rome. But if you think that was the end of Cleo's love life, think again—enter Mark Antony, one of Caesar's top generals and a swaggering power-player of his own. A few years later, Cleopatra set her sights on Antony, and she staged an introduction that makes the carpet incident look tame. In 41 BC, Cleopatra sailed to meet Mark Antony on her royal barge in a scene so extravagant it could make a Beyoncé concert look modest.

Gilded stern, purple sails, silver oars beating time to music, Cleopatra presented herself as the goddess Venus incarnate on a golden boat. The message was clear: the Queen of Egypt had arrived, and *she* was in charge of the narrative. Antony, a notorious lover of luxury and spectacle, didn't stand a chance. Like Caesar before him, he was captivated on the spot. Ancient historian Plutarch even wrote that Cleopatra's presence was "something bewitching," and that *"it was a pleasure merely to hear the sound of her voice"*. In modern terms, Cleopatra had serious charisma skills, the kind that makes powerful men forget reason and duty.

What followed was one of history's great power-couple sagas. Antony, one of the three rulers of the Roman Republic at the time, basically shirked his imperial responsibilities to spend a lost winter in Alexandria with Cleopatra. Imagine a top general today ghosting the Pentagon to vacation on a private island with his lover—that's the level of *dereliction of duty* we're talking about. Mark Antony left his wife (who inconveniently happened to be Octavian's sister, Octavia) waiting in Rome, parked his legions idle, and indulged in the high life with Cleopatra.

The pair formed their own mini-court of love and luxury; think of it as an ancient version of a celebrity power couple retreat, complete with feasting, wine, and late-night strategizing about how to rule the world (or at least the East). They even formed a blended family of sorts—Cleopatra gave birth to Antony's children (including twins, because of course this story needed more drama). Antony lavished Cleopatra with territories from Armenia to Cyprus as tokens of affection, in the infamous *Donations of Alexandria*. That was basically the ancient geopolitical equivalent of gifting your partner entire countries as love trinkets. (Hallmark, eat your heart out.) By now, Rome's establishment was in a frenzy, painting Antony as a traitor under the spell of a temptress. The affair of love versus duty had escalated into a full-blown political crisis.

It all led to war. *Love versus Empire: Round Two* – this time with Octavian (Julius Caesar's adoptive heir, later known as Augustus) pitted against Antony and Cleopatra. Octavian deftly spun the situation as a moral crusade: he portrayed Cleopatra as a foreign seductress corrupting a Roman noble, and Antony as a man who had "gone native" in decadent Alexandria.

In 31 BC, Octavian declared war – not on Antony (strategically, that might've been unpopular) but on *Cleopatra* herself. The showdown came at the Battle of Actium, a massive naval clash off the coast of Greece. It was a disaster for the star-crossed lovers: Antony and Cleopatra's forces were crushed by Octavian's fleet. The defeat spelled the end for them in more ways than one.

Back in Egypt, with Octavian closing in, the tragedy reached Shakespearean heights (literally—Shakespeare later dramatized this, but the real events were just as juicy). Mark Antony, hearing a (false) rumor that Cleopatra had committed suicide, fell on his sword in despair. Even *that* didn't go as planned: he survived the stab long enough to be carried to Cleopatra's hideout, and died in her arms. One can only imagine the heartbreak in that reunion—Antony bleeding, Cleopatra sobbing, both realizing the jig is up. With her partner gone and Octavian intent on parading her as a captive through the streets of Rome, Cleopatra chose a defiant exit.

The proud Egyptian queen famously took her own life rather than face humiliation—according to legend by pressing a venomous asp to her breast. Thus, in August 30 BC, Cleopatra died as she had lived: dramatically. With her death, Egypt fell to Rome, and 3,000 years of pharaohs officially came to an end. Octavian would go on to become Augustus, first emperor of Rome, and he made sure Cleopatra and Antony's children were either killed or paraded in chains as a warning that Rome bows to no love story.

Cleopatra's forbidden romances had upended the ancient world. In following her heart (and ambition), she won brief glory—an alliance with Caesar that shored up her throne, a passionate union with Antony that briefly made them co-rulers of the East. But the price was steep: her love affairs provoked civil wars and ultimately cost her everything. It's the classic theme of love versus duty, played out on a world stage. Cleopatra's passion both uplifted her (she secured her power through these liaisons in the short term) and unraveled her empire (Egypt was conquered as a direct result). To this day, we remember Cleopatra not just as a monarch, but as the woman who loved so boldly it shook the foundations of Rome. Her life has inspired countless works—from Plutarch's histories to modern films—precisely because it hits that irresistible storyline: love, power, transgression, and a dash of tragedy. If there's a clear lesson from Cleopatra's saga, it might be that mixing *business and pleasure* (or in her case, politics and passion) can change the course of history… but rarely without ruin.

(And for the record, yes, the whole carpet stunt likely happened—so next time someone says, "drop by anytime," consider taking a page from Cleopatra and make an entrance they'll never forget.)

Shah Jahan and Mumtaz Mahal: A Monumental Love (Mughal Empire)

Shifting from the Mediterranean melodrama, we turn to a love story from the Mughal Empire of India that is equal parts heartwarming and heart-wrenching. If Cleopatra's love brought down a dynasty, the love of Prince Khurram (better known by his regal name *Shah Jahan*) for Mumtaz Mahal built something *up*, specifically, one of the most stunning structures on Earth. You might have heard of it: a little building called the Taj Mahal. But behind that marble masterpiece lies a tale of passion, devotion, and the price an empire paid for one man's romantic obsession.

Our story begins around 1607 in Agra. Prince Khurram, a Mughal prince, caught sight of a young Persian noblewoman named Arjumand Banu Begum at the royal bazaar. It was love at first sight literally. The prince was so besotted that he went straight to his father, Emperor Jahangir, and declared his desire to marry her. They got engaged almost immediately (talk about *whirlwind romance*), though court astrologers made them wait five years to actually tie the knot (even true love had to align with the stars in those days). In 1612 they married, and Khurram gave his bride the title *Mumtaz Mahal*, meaning "Chosen One of the Palace".

By all accounts, their bond was extraordinarily deep. Remember, Shah Jahan (as Khurram would later be known) was a man entitled to multiple wives and he did have other wives for political reasons, but

Mumtaz was his clear favorite, his true partner in all things. She was beautiful and compassionate, but more importantly, she was his confidante and friend. Unlike many royal wives, Mumtaz accompanied Shah Jahan even on military campaigns, through dusty battlefields and distant provinces, never leaving his side.

Over 19 years of marriage, they had 14 children (yes, fourteen!), seven of whom survived past infancy. Amid the harems and pomp of Mughal court life, theirs was a genuine partnership. She advised him, soothed his temper, and by all evidence, never sought the limelight or political power for herself. If this were a movie, Mumtaz would be portrayed as the steady, beloved queen to Shah Jahan's emperor—a bit like a *Mughal Empire power couple* doing the 17th-century equivalent of state visits *and* date nights.

Tragedy struck in 1631. Mumtaz Mahal was accompanying Shah Jahan on a military campaign (one of his periodic attempts to expand or secure his realm) when she went into labor with their 14th child. The childbirth was arduous, and Mumtaz died in her husband's arms from complications. Shah Jahan was devastated. Legend has it that in his grief, the 36-year-old emperor's hair turned white overnight. While that might be apocryphal, there's no doubt he was absolutely shattered by her loss.

He went into secluded mourning for a long time, inconsolable and reportedly refusing to attend to the usual pleasures of the court. The emperor who had everything was now a widower who had lost his favorite part of himself. In a final promise, Shah Jahan vowed to build the most magnificent mausoleum for his beloved, so that the world would never forget their love. What followed is both a love letter in stone and a tale of royal obsession.

Shah Jahan threw himself into the project of commemorating Mumtaz. And by "project," we're talking about perhaps the grandest construction project of the age. The result, of course, was the Taj Mahal – often hailed as the ultimate monument to love. But building it was no simple task; it took 22 years of relentless work (1631–1653) and the resources of an empire. Shah Jahan effectively said, "Budget be damned, my love deserves perfection," and he meant it. He *spared no expense* in adorning this mausoleum with breathtaking detail. White marble from hundreds of miles away, inlaid gemstones from across Asia, intricate carvings and calligraphy, only the best for Mumtaz.

The workforce was colossal: historical accounts speak of over 20,000 workers laboring on the Taj, including artisans recruited from as far as Persia and Europe, plus around 1,000 elephants employed to haul materials. The empire's treasury poured into this singular edifice; heavy taxes were levied to fund it. (Imagine an entire nation's tax revenue diverted to building one giant tomb because the boss is heartbroken, now *that's* a flex, albeit a controversial one.) It's said that Shah Jahan's obsession with creating a flawless memorial was so consuming that it distracted him from governance.

The Mughal Empire was one of the richest in the world, but even so, such unrestrained spending and single-minded focus on a tomb was bound to cause some eye-rolling at court (and perhaps some nervous nail-biting among the accountants). Some historians even argue that the Taj Mahal project strained the Mughal treasury and contributed to the empire's fiscal decline. In the words of one modern historian, Shah Jahan's monument "became a monument to everlasting love but bankrupted the Mughal empire". That might be a bit of dramatic license, but it captures the idea that this was *love at a high cost.*

And Shah Jahan wasn't done dreaming. According to legend, he had an even more extravagant plan: he envisioned building a second Taj Mahal across the Yamuna River, identical to the first but made entirely of black marble, where he himself would be entombed. The idea was to have two grand mausoleums facing each other in mirror image, one white, one black, connected by a silver bridge. (Talk about *gilding the lily*—one Taj wasn't enough!).

This story of the "Black Taj" is likely a myth, born from later lore and the fact that the actual Taj Mahal complex is asymmetric (Shah Jahan's cenotaph is oddly placed to the side of Mumtaz's). But it's a compelling myth that speaks to how far Shah Jahan might have gone if he could. Obsessed with memorializing his love, he probably would have kept building, jewel-encrusting, and ornamenting forever if left unchecked.

However, Shah Jahan's romantic devotion carried a heavy price: it cost him his throne. While the emperor was busy playing architect-in-chief and grieving husband, the wheels of palace intrigue kept turning. His adult sons (he had many, but four in particular were vying for power) grew restless. The Mughal Empire valued strong leadership, and some at court whispered that Shah Jahan had taken his eye off the ball.

In 1658, his ambitious son Aurangzeb decided it was time for a coup. Aurangzeb gathered support, declared his father unfit to rule, and executed a swift takeover, eliminating his brothers in a brutal war of succession and seizing the Peacock Throne for himself. Shah Jahan was deposed by his own child; a palace coup fueled partly by the sense that the emperor had grown indulgent and neglectful of state affairs. The once-mighty ruler was placed under house arrest in the Red Fort of Agra. In a poetic yet heartbreaking twist, Shah Jahan's prison quarters had a direct view of the Taj Mahal.

The old emperor spent his final eight years confined, gazing out at the shining dome of the monument that symbolized his love, now also a reminder of the kingdom he'd *lost* for that love. When Shah Jahan died in 1666, Aurangzeb did allow him a final honor: the lovers were reunited in death, as Shah Jahan was laid to rest in the Taj Mahal next to Mumtaz, under the glorious dome he built for her.

Thus, the tale of Shah Jahan and Mumtaz Mahal embodies the double-edged nature of passion. On one hand, their love uplifted culture and art—giving the world a wonder that continues to awe millions. The Taj Mahal stands as an undying testament to how deeply one man cherished his wife; it's often called "a teardrop on the cheek of time," the ultimate declaration of love in stone.

On the other hand, that very passion unraveled the Mughal stability: it diverted attention and resources away from ruling an empire, created fissures in the royal family, and ushered in a more austere (and less culturally tolerant) era under Aurangzeb. Love versus duty was at the core of this saga too, though in a different way than Cleopatra's. Shah Jahan *had* the socially acceptable marriage, no one forbade him from loving Mumtaz, she was his legitimate wife. The "forbidden" aspect, if any, was the extent to which he allowed personal grief to override imperial duty. In a sense, his heart's desire became more important than his crown, and he paid the price.

Modern analogies almost fail to capture the scale of Shah Jahan's act. It's as if a modern leader today diverted the entire national budget to build a colossal memorial for their spouse—imagine a skyscraper made of gold dedicated to a lost love, while government business languishes. It sounds absurd, yet that's essentially what happened. And while most of us would agree that love is priceless, the Mughal courtiers circa 1650 might have preferred a slightly *cheaper* token of affection.

Still, one cannot help but be moved by the romance of it all. In a world of arranged marriages and political alliances, Shah Jahan and Mumtaz Mahal's genuine love story shines bright. Its legacy is quite literally etched in stone. Next time you see a photo of the Taj Mahal, perhaps with tourists posing and Instagramming away, remember that it was born from a forbidden level of devotion, a passion so powerful it built a paradise for the dead and nearly brought an empire to its knees.

King Edward VIII and Wallis Simpson: The King Who Abdicated for Love (United Kingdom)

For our final act, let's jump to the 20th century, where love's upheaval plays out not on a battlefield or in marble, but in the gleaming halls of Buckingham Palace. It's often called the abdication crisis of 1936, but it might as well be titled "Royal Bachelor: King Edition." The key players: King Edward VIII of Great Britain and a fashionable American socialite, Wallis Simpson. Their love story was *forbidden* in a very explicit way so much so that the king had to choose between his crown and his lady. Spoiler: he chose the lady. The result? A constitutional crisis that rocked the British monarchy and fascinated the world.

Edward VIII wasn't your typical duty-first monarch to begin with. Even before he met Wallis, he had a bit of a reputation as a free spirit and playboy prince. He was charming, stylish, and loved the high life, qualities that made him popular with the public, but a headache for those behind palace doors.

Enter Wallis Warfield Simpson: An American woman of modest origins, with two divorces under her belt and a sharp wit to match. Edward met Wallis around 1931 (when he was still just the Prince of Wales), and by the mid-1930s, they had fallen deeply in love. One small catch: Wallis was married (to husband number two) when their affair began, and even after she obtained a divorce, she would be a two-time divorcée seeking to marry the King of England. In the 1930s, that was a *huge* no-no. How huge? Let's put it this way: as King,

Edward VIII was also the nominal head of the Church of England, which at that time strictly forbade remarriage if a former spouse was still living. Wallis had not one but *two* living ex-husbands. The British establishment, government, church, press barons, you name it, found this prospect unacceptable. She was seen as politically and socially unsuitable to be queen, not to mention the moral outrage from those who deemed her a twice-divorced American adventuress.

The Prime Minister, Stanley Baldwin, and his cabinet were adamant: if Edward insisted on marrying Wallis, it would trigger the government's resignation and a national crisis. The governments of the British Commonwealth (Canada, Australia, etc.) echoed that disapproval. In short, virtually the entire apparatus of empire told Edward, "It's *her* or the throne, you can't have both."

This conflict between love and duty built throughout 1936, which also happened to be the first year of Edward's reign (he became king in January 1936 after his father George V died). So, picture this: the poor guy had only just started the top job when he was confronted with the choice of a lifetime. Usually, fairy tales have a prince giving up love to become king; here we had a king willing to give up being king to have his love. It was unprecedented.

The British public by and large had no clue what was brewing for most of the year, there was actually a press blackout in the UK about Edward's relationship with Wallis, even though foreign newspapers were filled with it. (Yes, amazingly, British media once collectively agreed to *not* publish juicy gossip about the royals, imagine trying to pull that off in the age of Twitter!) By autumn 1936, Wallis's second divorce was nearing completion, and Edward was pushing hard to make Wallis his wife and queen. The establishment pushed back with equal force. Something had to give.

In December 1936, the crisis came to a head. Edward proposed a solution: a morganatic marriage, where he'd remain king, but Wallis would not be given the title of Queen. This was rejected by the government. Facing intense pressure, Edward made a decision that stunned the world: he chose Wallis. On December 11, 1936, King Edward VIII became the first English monarch ever to voluntarily abdicate the throne because of a personal desire. In a radio broadcast that evening, he addressed his nation (now as *Prince* Edward, since by then his younger brother had been proclaimed George VI) and poured his heart out.

In the most famous line from that speech, he explained that he found it impossible to carry the heavy burden of kingship "without the help and support of the woman I love." It was a moment of high romance and high drama, listeners around the globe were astonished. A king giving it all up for love? It was the stuff of legend, happening live on the airwaves. This was not some ancient fable; it was playing out in real time, covered by newsreels and newspapers worldwide. As the BBC later described it, Edward's abdication "tested the boundaries of duty, love and the monarchy itself".

And just like that, the love-struck king was demoted to a royal footnote. Edward VIII's reign had lasted only 327 days, but his love for Wallis would last the rest of his life. He was succeeded by his stammering, younger brother Albert (George VI), who had to step up and patch the cracks in the monarchy, *talk about an awkward first day at work* for George, who never wanted the crown. (If you've seen the film *The King's Speech*, you know how that went: the shy duke with a speech impediment suddenly has to rally an empire because his brother fell in love. Truth really is stranger than fiction.) Edward, now given the title Duke of Windsor, married Wallis Simpson in 1937 in a small private ceremony in France. Not one member of the royal family attended, the wounds were still fresh.

The two lovebirds then essentially lived in exile, splitting time between Europe and the Bahamas (where Edward had a stint as Governor during World War II). They became society celebrities, always good for a stylish photograph in magazines, yet they were forever shadowed by the abdication fallout and, controversially, by their cozy relations with Nazi Germany (they infamously met Hitler in 1937, giving *fodder* to critics who said maybe Britain was better off without this pair in charge).

The British establishment, for its part, breathed a sigh of relief that the "crisis" was over, but the monarchy had been irrevocably changed. Queen Elizabeth (the Queen Mother) reportedly referred to Wallis as "that woman" for decades, reflecting the family's scorn. As a concession, Edward got a comfortable allowance and kept his Royal Highness style, but Wallis was pointedly denied "Her Royal Highness" status. It was a royal cold shoulder if ever there was one.

Public opinion at the time of the abdication was mixed. Some Britons were outraged that Edward would abandon his duty, especially on the eve of World War II, when stable leadership was crucial. Others found it wildly romantic that he'd sacrifice the crown for love. In the decades since, the verdict on Edward and Wallis has seesawed. Some view them as a couple who bravely followed their hearts; others see a feckless king and an ambitious woman whose choices could have endangered the monarchy.

One thing's for sure: their story is addictive. It has inspired countless books, movies, and TV shows (chances are you've seen their fictional counterparts in *The Crown* or some BBC drama). Why? Because it perfectly encapsulates the tension of personal desire versus public duty. Edward VIII, born and bred to be king, shocked everyone by saying, "Actually… I choose love." The allure of transgression—an English king marrying an American divorcée—was so strong that he upended centuries of tradition.

In a sense, this was *forbidden love* in the social-religious context of the day, and it proved powerful enough to alter the line of succession of the British royal family. The personal risk Edward took was enormous: he exchanged the literal crown on his head for an uncertain future with the woman he adored.

So, did passion uplift or unravel here? In the short term, it rather unraveled the orderly plan for the monarchy. Britain got a new king it hadn't expected, and Edward and Wallis were ostracized. But arguably, it also uplifted the narrative of love in the modern era—suddenly, here was a living example that *true love* might be worth the highest sacrifice. Many romantics at the time (and since) have swooned over the idea. Culturally, it's had lasting appeal: just think how often we still hear the phrase "the woman I love" associated with Edward VIII as a symbol of devotion.

Interestingly, the monarchy survived and even strengthened in the aftermath under George VI and then the long reign of his daughter Elizabeth II. In fact, one could say Edward's abdication indirectly paved the way for a more modern monarchy down the line (one that, with much kicking and screaming, eventually tolerated a King marrying a divorcée—hello, Charles and Camilla). But that's another story. The tale of Edward and Wallis stands on its own as a poignant example of the heart trumping the crown. It's essentially the royal version of "love wins," albeit with asterisk conditions and fine print.

Interpretation and Moral Lesson:
The Price of Desire: Love vs Duty and the Allure of Transgression

What do these three tales separated by centuries have in common? In each, passion collided head-on with responsibility, and the fallout was spectacular. They are case studies in the timeless tension between following one's heart and fulfilling one's duty. These romances were "forbidden" not always in the same way. Cleopatra's loves were forbidden by political rivalry, Shah Jahan's obsessive mourning broke the unwritten rules of prudent governance, and Edward VIII's marriage violated the social and religious codes of his era.

Yet, in all three, the lovers knew they were venturing beyond what was acceptable or safe, and that very forbidden quality likely fanned the flames of desire. There's a certain *allure of transgression* when you risk a kingdom (or at least a crown) to be with someone. It's the stuff of legend and pop culture alike: the idea that love is worth any price. But our stories also show the other side of that coin: the price *can* be steep indeed.

In Cleopatra's case, following her heart (and political instincts) with Caesar and Antony initially elevated her status, she secured her throne, enjoyed great power, and lived in legendary luxury. But in the end, her passion literally unraveled empires: the Roman Republic turned into an Empire under Augustus as a direct outcome of the war sparked by her love affair, and the ancient Pharaohs' rule in Egypt came to a permanent close.

For Shah Jahan, his unyielding love built something eternally beautiful, the Taj Mahal's white dome may be the most uplifting symbol of love on Earth. Yet that same love-led obsession weakened his rule and hastened his downfall; the Mughal Empire would never quite be the same after the turmoil that his neglect (and his son's usurpation) brought. And for Edward VIII, the choice of love over duty gave him personal happiness (by most accounts he and Wallis remained devoted to each other for life), but it *cost him his kingdom.*

His personal life flourished in exile, but his public role was reduced to nearly nothing; he went from King-Emperor to an aimless socialite, forever remembered as the monarch who quit. In each story, passion both uplifted and undermined: it created legacies (cultural or personal) that inspire us, while also causing collateral damage in the form of political chaos or decline.

There is a clear moral thread weaving through these tales: the personal risks of following the heart can be enormous, especially for those in power. Love, that most human of emotions, doesn't bow to titles or borders. When a ruler's heart is given away, the whole realm often feels the tremors.

The "forbidden" aspect, be it taboo love, obsessive grief, or defiance of protocol, adds fuel to the fire, making the passion all the more intense and history-making. It's as if the universe can't help but take notice when a king, queen, or emperor says, "To heck with the rules, I choose love." Such choices can inspire awe (we still marvel at the romance) and anxiety (we witness the fallout).

In a modern context, we're still fascinated by these stories because they're relatable yet larger-than-life. We've all had to make choices between what we desire and what is expected of us, though usually on a much smaller scale than, say, choosing between an empire and a soulmate. The stakes for these historical figures were stratospheric, which is why their decisions echo through time. They remind us that the people in the portraits and history books were, in the end, people, vulnerable to love's call, just like anyone else. Cleopatra, Shah Jahan, Edward VIII – they might have worn crowns, but their hearts weren't invincible.

The clear takeaway? Passion is powerful. It can drive people to extraordinary achievements and to devastating falls. It can uplift, producing timeless art, legendary tales, even altering the course of nations in positive ways and it can unravel, leading to loss, conflict, and the end of eras. As we close this chapter on forbidden love and the price of desire, perhaps the final lesson is a balanced one: follow your heart, yes, but tread carefully if the whole kingdom is following *you.*

History's lovestruck royals followed their hearts right off the map of the known world, and while we wouldn't have it any less dramatic (who doesn't love a good story?), it certainly wasn't *happily ever after* in the conventional sense. Instead, their legacies live on as cautionary tales and eternal romances entwined. In the grand tapestry of history, these passionate affairs leave an indelible pattern: hearts set ablaze can illuminate the world or burn it down. The difference often lies in that razor's edge between love and duty, a line every leader must navigate, and one that these three couples daringly crossed.

So, the next time you hear a phrase like "all for love," think of Cleopatra, Shah Jahan, and Edward VIII. They *literally* moved mountains (or built them) for love and faced the consequences. Their stories, full of wit, wonder, and woe, continue to captivate us, reminding us that the power of passion is a force to reckon with, one that even empires must yield to, for better or for worse.

Chapter 2

Marriages of State—
Love as a Political Strategy

Marrying for love? How adorably modern. For much of history, marriage was less about finding *the one* and more about finding the right one – the one with the proper royal lineage, alliance value, or a sizable army to back up the wedding vows. In other words, love often took a backseat while politics rode shotgun. Picture a medieval wedding as a high-stakes chess move, or better yet, a corporate merger with **"I do"**s.

It's the stuff of dynastic unity, empire-building, and the erasure of personal will – served with a side of cake (sometimes) and a wink to Cupid. And if you think your family gatherings are awkward, imagine being the poor bride or groom traded like a collectible card to secure a peace treaty. Before diving into three famous tales; Ferdinand and Isabella of Spain, Marie Antoinette and Louis XVI of France, and the Goryeo princesses in the Mongol Empire, let's set the scene with a bit of humor (because trust us, the reality was heavy, so we'll need the laughs):

- No Pressure, It's Just World Peace: Often a teenager would wake up betrothed to a stranger to end a war. (Beats fighting on the battlefield, but still – yikes.)

- In-Laws of the Realm: Your new spouse's family might literally *be* the neighboring kingdom. In-laws with armies – what could go wrong?
- Love Optional (Strictly Business): Affection was nice if it blossomed, but it wasn't the point. When kingdoms were on the line, personal choice was collateral damage.

These "altar diplomacy" deals were the Game of Thrones of the real world (minus the dragons, plus actual paperwork). Even Disney has toyed with the trope, remember Princess Jasmine protesting an arranged marriage in *Aladdin*? In real life, Jasmines rarely had a pet tiger or a friendly genie to bail them out. Instead, they had duty, diplomatic cables, and sometimes a quill-signed treaty. In this chapter, we'll tour some lavish yet loveless (or at least *strategic*) unions that shaped history, all while casting a wry eye on the human cost of turning hearts into bargaining chips.

Ferdinand and Isabella – A Match Made in... Aragon? Castile? (Spain's Power Couple)

Ferdinand of Aragon and Isabella of Castile, whose union in 1469 brought two kingdoms together. Their marriage, while not sparked by passion at first sight, became one of history's most successful power partnerships.

In 1469, an 18-year-old princess from Castile and a 17-year-old prince from Aragon met for the very first time, and within a week, *bam!* they were married. Forget long courtships; when uniting two major realms of Spain was at stake, speed was of the essence. This wasn't exactly a fairy-tale romance where they locked eyes across a crowded throne room. In fact, "this was not a love-match; the two had never even met and it was a highly choreographed political union". Both Isabella I of Castile and Ferdinand II of Aragon knew exactly what they were doing: choosing a spouse as a conscious political strategy, not because a love arrow had struck them in the heart.

To call their wedding planning *dramatic* is an understatement. Isabella's half-brother, King Henry IV of Castile, was against the match (he had other plans for her hand), so the young princess literally snuck out under the pretext of visiting her brother's tomb, a classic *"BRB, just going to pay respects"* excuse – and hightailed it to meet Ferdinand in secret. Meanwhile, Prince Ferdinand had his own incognito adventure: he traveled across Castile disguised as a servant to avoid detection. Cue the rom-com montage of the prince in shabby clothes sneaking past castle guards – it's like a medieval *Meet-cute* with a touch of *Mission: Impossible*. They tied the knot in a small private ceremony that October, effectively thumbing their noses at the naysayers in high places.

Of course, there was one *teensy* problem; the Catholic Church forbade marriages between close cousins, and Ferdinand and Isabella were second cousins. No issue: they simply procured a papal dispensation to waive the rules. How? Let's just say the paperwork was *questionable* – rumor has it the dispensation was signed by a Pope who had already been dead for five years, likely a forged favor cooked up by Ferdinand's dad and a well-placed Church ally. (If that's not bending the rules with divine paperwork, what is?) When you're engineering the unification of Spain, apparently even the laws of consanguinity can be massaged.

From the get-go, Ferdinand and Isabella treated their marriage like a merger of equals – well, mostly equals. They negotiated terms in a prenuptial treaty called the Capitulations of Cervera, which was read aloud at the wedding for good measure. Picture it: a priest, a few witnesses, and someone reciting the fine print that basically said *"Isabella gets to rule Castile and Aragon as Queen, Ferdinand is her consort, and Castile will be the dominant partner"*. Nothing says romance like a contract signing at the altar!

It was crystal clear this was a business deal between kingdoms as much as a union of two people. In fact, Isabella didn't even inform her kingly brother; she went rogue. When Henry IV found out his little sister married the Aragonese heir behind his back, he was livid ; he disinherited her in favor of his own daughter (throwing shade that the girl was illegitimate, calling her *"la Beltraneja"*, but that's another soap opera).

So why all this subterfuge and plotting? Because this marriage was basically the *Iberian Union 1.0.* By getting hitched, Isabella and Ferdinand set in motion the de facto unification of Spain. They were later dubbed the "Catholic Monarchs" for their zeal in defending the faith (and perhaps for staying married to each other for over 30 years, a feat in itself). Their partnership created a dynastic alliance that brought Castile and Aragon under one family, laying the groundwork for a single Spanish monarchy. Scholars often trace *the birth of a unified Spain* directly back to this marriage. Basically, they formed a power couple Avant la lettre; the original hashtag might have been #Ferdabella if medieval Twitter existed.

To be fair, for a pair that married for strategy, Ferdinand and Isabella ended up getting along remarkably well. They worked in tandem and presented a united front, both aware that *"the crown of Castile was the prize, and they were jointly gambling for it"*. Over time, theirs became a "remarkably successful political partnership and personal relationship" Imagine that a marriage arranged for politics that didn't end in misery or endless court feuds, but actually in mutual respect (and a bunch of kids to marry off in their turn).

They coordinated military campaigns and reforms, and together they completed the *Reconquista* (ousting the last Muslim kingdom of Granada in 1492), achieving in partnership what neither could alone. If this were a movie, it's the part where the initially awkward couple realizes they make a great team. (Move over, *Bridgerton*, these two were doing "power marriage" before it was cool.)

Dynastic unity was only the beginning. With their realms combined, Ferdinand and Isabella looked outward. In the same fateful year of 1492, Queen Isabella decided to sponsor a Genoese explorer named Columbus – you might have heard of him – to find a westward route to Asia. Ferdinand was busy elsewhere, so Isabella largely funded this gamble herself, and when Columbus instead bumped into the Americas, all that glory (and eventual wealth) flowed into Castile's coffers. It was the kickoff to Spain's global empire, which would make it the superpower of Europe for the next century and more. Not a bad outcome for a marriage that started as a cloak-and-dagger elopement with legal forgery on the side. Together they effectively said, *"Today: Spain, Tomorrow: the world."*

Of course, not everything was sunshine and roses. Their joint reign also gave us the Spanish Inquisition (surprise! no one expects it – not even newlyweds), and the expulsion of Jews and Muslims from Spain. While those policies were framed in religious terms, they were also about cementing their control – forging one faith to strengthen one state. It's a stark reminder that even as we crack jokes about treaties at the altar, the political power they wielded had very real human consequences. Isabella and Ferdinand's love story (if we can call it that) was one written in iron will and ink, not exactly poetry. Yet, in an ironic twist, their marriage did manage to blend strategy and a bit of genuine partnership. They proved that sometimes two people can start as pawns in a game of thrones, and end up as players, albeit at a cost.

Before we leave our Spanish power couple, let's appreciate the imagery: the royal pair touring their kingdoms on muleback (they couldn't Instagram their progress, so they physically showed up to win loyalty), raising five children whom they married off all across Europe like diplomatic chess pieces. (Their daughter Catherine of Aragon, for one, became the first wife of Henry VIII of England – and you know how that one ended. Divorce, beheaded... well, story for another chapter.) Ferdinand and Isabella were effectively the CEOs of "Spain, Inc.," leveraging matrimony as a tool to build a brand-new nation.

It's no wonder that a later royal observer coined the saying: "Let others wage war; you, fortunate Austria, marry!" – a nod to how powerful families like the Habsburgs preferred forging power through dynastic marriages rather than battles. Our Spanish duo would probably nod in agreement; they united crowns first, then used that unity to unleash forces that changed the world.

Marie Antoinette and Louis XVI –: The Alliance That Lost Its Head (Literally)

An 18th-century engraving celebrating the wedding of the Dauphin Louis (future Louis XVI) and Archduchess Marie Antoinette of Austria in 1770. This political marriage was a glittering spectacle, and an alliance sealed with a ring (and a hefty side of diplomatic baggage).

Fast forward a few centuries to another teenage bride, another political deal. This time, we're in 1770s France, with powdered wigs, courtiers, and a marriage that was supposed to secure peace but ended up capped by the guillotine. Marie Antoinette, the 14-year-old daughter of Empress Maria Theresa of Austria, was shipped off to France to marry the 15-year-old Louis-Auguste, the Dauphin (heir) of France, who would become Louis XVI.

If Ferdinand and Isabella's union created a world empire, Marie and Louis's union previewed a world of trouble. Their marriage was the result of the Diplomatic Revolution of 1756, a fancy term for when old enemies France and Austria became pals against Prussia and England. And how do you cement such an unlikely friendship? *"Seal their alliance with a marriage,"* of course. In 1770, Louis XV of France (Louis XVI's grandpa) formally *"asked the hand"* of young Archduchess Maria Antonia for his grandson.

This was a carefully orchestrated union joining the Austrian Habsburgs and the French Bourbons, the two most powerful dynasties around, and teenage Marie was, as one commentator put it, *"nothing more than a bargaining chip for her mother."*

Think about that: at 10 years old, Marie Antoinette was basically signed up for a future she had no say in (Meanwhile, at 10 we were trading Pokémon cards, not being traded *as* a diplomatic card.) By the time she was 14, she was saying "oui" in a grand ceremony at Versailles, decked in jewels and silks with 5,000 guests watching every move. Talk about a high-pressure wedding ; even *Bridgerton* would blush. In a symbolic (and rather cruel) gesture, Marie had to renounce all her rights to her Austrian heritage before crossing into France.

They literally stripped her of everything Austrian at the border – : clothes, name (she became "Marie Antoinette" instead of Maria Antonia) – to transform her into the future French queen. It was a full identity swap for the sake of alliance: one day she's an Austrian princess with a pet pug and a musical education, the next she's the Dauphine of France, expected to eventually produce an heir and solidify the Franco-Austrian bond. No pressure, right?

To say this was *not* a love marriage is putting it mildly. "It was not a marriage of love. Merely a strategic union," as one historian dryly noted of Louis and Marie's nuptials. The teens had only a vague idea of each other (they were actually second cousins, but who's counting?). On their wedding night, tradition had a crowd of courtiers accompany them to the royal bedchamber – yes, as in *watch them go to bed* – then wait eagerly for… well, confirmation of *amorous success*. Talk about performance anxiety! It turns out our young couple didn't quite know what to do with each other in private, and the anticipated consummation did not happen for seven years.

Cue the 18th-century gossip mill: pamphlets and scandalous jokes circulated widely, mocking the royal pair's intimate ineptitude. (Think of it as the TMZ of Versailles, spreading "news" that the marriage wasn't *officially official* yet.) Eventually, likely after some *ahem* advice and possibly minor medical intervention for Louis, they managed to fulfill their duty in 1777, and kids followed. But those early years of awkward silence in the bedroom symbolized the bigger issue: this was an alliance in name long before it became a bond in heart.

The political rationale behind this marriage was sound on paper. France and Austria had been enemies for ages, but after being thrashed in the Seven Years' War, both courts thought, *"Hey, maybe we should team up instead."* Empress Maria Theresa and King Louis XV wanted to "destroy the ambitions of Prussia and Great Britain", and nothing says BFFs like exchanging children in matrimony. As a result, young Marie Antoinette became the living embodiment of the Franco-Austrian alliance – a walking, talking (eventually cake-eating) peace treaty in a pannier dress.

However, unlike in Spain where the union was popular, in France many were *not* on board with this new friendship. The French public basically went, *"We bled and lost wars because of Austria, and now we're marrying one? C'est quoi ça?!"* Indeed, France's alliance with Austria had dragged it into that disastrous Seven Years' War, and folks hadn't forgotten. When Marie Antoinette arrived, she was met with both curiosity and skepticism. Some found her beautiful and charming at first (her 1773 public debut in Paris was a hit, go figure), but many others saw her as l'Autrichienne – literally "the Austrian woman," which in French sounds a bit like a slur – an unwelcome foreign princess foisted on them.

As time passed, the alliance that Marie represented started to lose its luster. Sure, for a while, things were okay: France and Austria maintained their détente, and Marie tried to play the part of a dutiful French queen-to-be. She even wrote letters back home that read like diplomatic dispatches (with her formidable mother Maria Theresa scrutinizing her behavior from afar – talk about helicopter parenting at a geopolitical scale). But being a teenager in the most extravagant, gossipy court in Europe had its pitfalls. Marie Antoinette, free from her mom's immediate supervision for the first time, indulged in the opulence of Versailles. She became a fashion trendsetter – with sky-high hairstyles and spending sprees that would make any shopaholic proud (or horrified, if you were the finance minister).

While her spending on gowns and gambling was actually a fraction of France's budget issues, she quickly became the scapegoat for everything wrong in France. Here's the cruel irony: Marie's marriage was meant to secure political harmony, but as France's economy faltered and the populace grew restless, people zeroed in on her foreign-ness and extravagance as symbols of a corrupt alliance. They coined nasty nicknames like "Madame Déficit," implying her Austrian ways and fancy lifestyle were draining France dry.

And then, of course, came the French Revolution. By 1789, any goodwill from the alliance was ancient history. Austria was seen less as an ally and more as a meddling power (especially when Marie's brother, Emperor Joseph II, and later Leopold II, threatened to intervene in French affairs to protect the royal family). To revolutionary eyes, Marie Antoinette was effectively an enemy agent – a Marie 007, if you will, but with way better dresses. The very marriage that was supposed to bond nations now painted the king and queen as traitors in some patriots' view. "Austrians at court" became a paranoid trope.

One could say love (or the appearance of it) became collateral damage in diplomacy: Marie's personal fate was sealed as much by her birth and marriage as by anything she did. In a darkly poetic turn, the same country that once celebrated her high-profile wedding now sentenced her to death as an embodiment of the hated old regime. In October 1793, Marie Antoinette was executed by guillotine – the revolutionary crowd even cheered as her head was displayed. So much for happily ever after.

From a moral lens, the story of Marie Antoinette and Louis XVI underscores the human cost of political consolidation through marriage. Marie had virtually no personal agency; she was groomed (literally and figuratively) to be a piece on Europe's chessboard. As one historian noted, she "had very little say in the conditions of her life". The alliance did bring a brief period of peace between France and Austria – Louis and Marie didn't personally start any wars with Austria, that's for sure – but it was peace built on a shaky foundation.

The people of France never truly accepted this foreign queen, and when starvation and inequality reached a boiling point, her symbolic role as an Austrian alliance pawn made her an easy target. Love? There might have been some genuine affection between Louis and Marie in their later years (some accounts say they grew close, especially as they faced imprisonment and death together). But in the ledger of diplomatic gains and losses, their love was, as our chapter title suggests, *collateral*. The alliance outlived its usefulness, and when the political winds shifted, the once-prized bride became a liability.

On a lighter note (we need one after that grim ending), modern pop culture has tried to rehabilitate Marie Antoinette a bit. Films like Sofia Coppola's *Marie Antoinette* portray her as a spirited young woman trapped by circumstances – essentially a kid who wanted to have fun but was handed a kingdom's burdens. It's a sympathetic spin that underscores our point: behind the grandeur of state marriages were often teenagers who would probably have preferred a normal life (or at least a less tragic one).

If Instagram existed in the 1770s, Marie might've been an influencer posting cake recipes and outfit pics, not a political scapegoat. But she lived in an age when marriage was diplomacy by other means, and for that she paid the ultimate price. The alliance that her marriage was meant to strengthen did not save her in the end – it merely set the stage for a very public, very tragic finale.

Goryeo Princesses and Mongol Khans – Korea's Game of Thrones Diplomacy

We've seen how marriage could unite huge European empires or entangle superpower alliances, but the concept wasn't exclusive to the West. In medieval Asia, similar dramas unfolded – perhaps none more intriguing (and at times jaw-dropping) than the matrimonial diplomacy between Korea's Goryeo dynasty and the mighty Mongol Yuan dynasty of China.

Think of it as an East Asian twist on "marriage as statecraft," complete with captive princesses, hostage grooms, and imperial in-laws so intimidating you *really* didn't want to forget their birthdays.

In the 13th century, the Mongol Empire was on a world-conquering spree (as Mongols do), and Korea's Goryeo kingdom was in their path. After decades of resistance and six devastating invasions, Goryeo finally capitulated in the 1270s. Now, Mongols aren't exactly known for tender peacemaking, but they did have a policy for dealing with troublesome neighbors: incorporate them into the family – by force if necessary. Goryeo became a vassal state of the

Yuan dynasty, and to ensure loyalty, the Mongol Khans and Goryeo kings started swapping sons and daughters like trading cards.

This earned Goryeo a peculiar nickname: a "son-in-law kingdom" of the Mongol Empire. Why "son-in-law"? Because so many Goryeo royalty either *married* or *were married to* Mongols that family trees started looking like tangled ivy. The Goryeo kings effectively became imperial sons-in-law (khuregen) to the Mongol Khans, entwining the Korean royal line with Genghis Khan's descendants. It was a classic *keep your friends close and your vassals closer* strategy.

Here's how it worked in practice: The Mongol Yuan court and the Goryeo court "exchanged princesses" as if arranging a very high-stakes playdate. Goryeo kings were required to marry Mongol princesses, and in return, Mongol princes (and aristocrats) received Goryeo brides. Basically, each side had a stake in the other's lineage. Beginning with King Chungnyeol of Goryeo marrying a daughter of Kublai Khan (yes, the famous Kublai, Genghis's grandson), there was a parade of royal intermarriages.

In total, eight Mongol princesses married into the Goryeo royal family – imagine eight consecutive queens all being born in the Great Khan's homeland. Those queens brought with them Mongol names, fashions, and yes, expectations. For example, any son born to a Mongol princess had a better claim to the Goryeo throne than sons from a Korean mother. The Mongols wanted to ensure that Goryeo's future kings were their *grandchildren* – talk about future-proofing your domination! One Goryeo prince not born of a Mongol mother was even disqualified from succession and exiled because his mom wasn't a Yuan princess. Harsh.

On the flip side, Korean women were sent to the Yuan court as well, sometimes as official brides for Mongol royalty, other times as concubines or "tribute women." In fact, the practice started quite grimly: Korean women entered the Mongol empire initially as war booty. Later, the Mongol elite got a taste for Goryeo brides and demanded a regular supply. Goryeo's kings balked at first, but eventually even set up a government office to select and send tribute women to the Mongol Empire.

It's as awful as it sounds – noble families in Goryeo had to contribute daughters to be shipped off to Mongolia/China as part of the "alliance." Over the decades, nearly 1,500 Korean women (recorded) were sent, though the real numbers may have been higher. Some became servants or ladies-in-waiting, but a few hit the jackpot (so to speak) by catching the eye of the Emperor himself.

The most famous of these was Lady Gi (or Empress Ki), a Goryeo-born woman who was sent to Yuan around 1333. She was a teenager, beautiful, and highly educated in the arts – basically prime candidate material for imperial favor. Sure enough, she "quickly became the favorite concubine" of Emperor Toghon Temür, the Mongol ruler of the Yuan at the time.

The Emperor fell in love with Lady Gi, preferring her company far above his official first wife. In a twist that no doubt shocked the stiff conservative court, he wanted to make this *Korean teenager* his secondary Empress – something unheard of, since traditionally only Mongol noblewomen got to be Empresses. The court officials were scandalized and tried to block it, but eventually Lady Gi did become Empress (and not just any Empress – she essentially ruled the Yuan

Empire from behind the scenes in its final years). She gave birth to a son who became the next Khan, securing her power.

Talk about playing the long game: a girl shipped off as a diplomatic offering ends up effectively running an empire of millions. If HBO hasn't made a series about her yet, they should – the *palace intrigue level* is off the charts.

Empress Gi's story is exceptional (and yes, there's a hit Korean TV drama called "Empress Ki" that romanticizes her life, complete with all the court scheming and doomed love – highly recommended for drama fans!). But many other Goryeo women likely led less glorious lives in the Yuan court. Some were married to Mongol princes, others to high officials.

By all accounts, it became "prestigious to marry Goryeo women" among the Mongol elite – almost a status symbol, because these women were renowned for their beauty and cultural sophistication. In a weird way, this *soft power* benefited Goryeo: Korean cuisine, clothing, and styles became trendy in Yuan thanks to these women bringing a bit of home with them. (K-culture wave, 13th-century edition!) But let's not sugarcoat it: they were essentially hostages turned trendsetters.

The personal cost was immense. Imagine being a Goryeo princess or noblewoman, sent far away from everything you know, to marry a foreign stranger in a land where if you don't please your husband (or the Emperor), your whole family back home could suffer. Love? That was a luxury few could afford in these circumstances. One Goryeo princess-turned-queen in Mongolia might have written letters home, but she couldn't exactly hop on a boat back if things got rough.

The marriages in the Goryeo-Mongol alliance also led to some *absurdly personal diplomatic crises.* Case in point: one Goryeo king, Chungseon, was married to a Yuan Mongol princess named Botashirin. Let's just say, he wasn't feeling it. He refused to consummate the marriage – repeatedly – preferring his Korean concubines instead. Princess Botashirin was not amused and did what any frustrated princess might do: she tattled to her grandpa, the Yuan Emperor.

The Mongol Empress Dowager even dispatched an envoy to Goryeo with a very awkward royal order: *tell the king to do his husbandly duty!* (We can only imagine the envoy's face delivering that message.) Chungseon still wouldn't oblige, which sparked such a scandal that ultimately he was deposed for fear that if Botashirin had a lover and a child, that half-Mongol baby might usurp the throne. The solution? Yuan sent poor Botashirin back and essentially fired the King of Goryeo for non-compliance. It's possibly the only time in history a monarch lost his crown for *not* sleeping with his wife. When we talk about the erasure of personal will – well, Chungseon tried to exert his will and learned there's no such thing as "not tonight, dear" when the fate of a kingdom hangs in the balance.

Ultimately, the Korea-Mongol marriage alliance era lasted about 80 years. It ended when the Mongol Yuan dynasty started crumbling in the 1350s and Goryeo's King Gongmin saw a chance to shake off the yoke. Gongmin, interestingly, had a Mongol wife (Queen Noguk) whom he reportedly loved deeply – so much so that after she died, he fell into madness. Even in these political marriages, you occasionally find a genuine human bond. But their story, too, is tinged with tragedy; they lost their only baby, and she died in childbirth. It's as if the universe kept reminding these royals: you can mix love and politics, but it's not a stable concoction.

From a moral standpoint, the Goryeo-Yuan marriages highlight how empire-building often literally went through the bedroom, and how *love, consent, and personal happiness were often sacrificed on the altar of state security.* Goryeo's royal family sometimes tried to resist – one king reportedly fled to the mountains rather than hand over his daughter – but in the end, the Mongol influence won.

The individuals involved, especially the young women, had little choice. Some, like Empress Gi, made the most of it and grabbed power for themselves (perhaps turning the tables on those who sought to use them). Many others vanish from the pages of history, known only by a line like "Married Princess So-and-So to Prince X." But their fate was shared by countless nameless others.

Conclusion: Love as Collateral Damage in the Chess Game of Thrones

Surveying these stories – from Spain's savvy monarchs to France's ill-fated royals, to Korea's reluctant princess emissaries – a clear theme emerges : marriage was a weapon in the arsenal of kings and queens, as critical as any sword or treaty. It was cheaper than war (usually), and had the bonus of creating *in-laws instead of enemies.* As a result, thrones were bolted together with wedding bands. But what about the brides and grooms? The human hearts beating under those heavy crowns?

In all these cases, love – genuine personal affection – was often incidental or even irrelevant to the match. Ferdinand and Isabella grew to respect and maybe love each other, but they entered into marriage eyes-wide-open for power. Marie Antoinette and Louis XVI *might* have eventually forged some fondness (shared trauma can do that), but they started as awkward strangers forced under the same canopy, and their marriage became a political powder keg that blew up in their faces. The Goryeo and Mongol unions were explicitly transactional: a cycle of "I'll give you my daughter, you give me peace (or at least don't invade again)."

What is striking is the moral calculus at play. These marriages of state present a sort of cold equation: *How many individual lives is it worth to secure a dynasty or avert a war?* To a king or queen, marrying off a child for alliance could save tens of thousands of lives on the battlefield. By that logic, the sacrifice of two unhappy people was a small price for stability. And indeed, sometimes it did work – Spain was unified, France and Austria had a lasting peace until the revolution, Goryeo survived under Mongol shadow without being totally annexed. Dynastic unity and empire-building were achieved, in large part, by turning princes and princesses into living pawns.

Yet, as we've also seen, the bill for using "love" as a bargaining chip comes due eventually. The pain of those in the arranged marriage can translate into bigger problems: a disconnected queen seen as "foreign" might become a focus of public anger (hello, Marie Antoinette). A king forced to marry someone he hates might rebel in dangerous ways (King Chungseon's little bedroom strike nearly caused a succession crisis). Even when the strategy succeeds politically, there's often a human tragedy lurking: lost youth, homesickness, loveless partnerships, early deaths. The heart doesn't always obey the state.

To wrap up on a conversational (and slightly humorous) note: one could say history is full of "It's complicated" relationship statuses when it comes to royal romances. Think of these tales next time you hear about a celebrity "power couple" – at least those folks usually choose each other and only merge their brands, not their sovereign realms. Modern royals, too, largely marry for love these days, precisely because we've recognized that people aren't chess pieces. The stories in this chapter serve as both fascinating drama and cautionary tale. They invite us to empathize with those young brides and grooms who bore the weight of nations on their shoulders (or, more literally, in their marriage beds).

In the grand moral ledger, using marriage as a political strategy often meant stealing the personal freedom of a few to (supposedly) benefit the many. Love, in these scenarios, was collateral damage – sometimes it blossomed in spite of everything (as perhaps with Ferdinand and Isabel, but more often it was a ghost at the feast, overshadowed by duty, ambition, and survival.

So, what do we learn from these "marriages of state"? Perhaps this: If you treat love as a tool rather than a truth, don't be surprised when the tool breaks or backfires. The alliances may crumble, the empires may fall, but the personal costs – the lonely queens, the exiled princesses, the executed royals – remain long after in the pages of history. In the end, history's great power couples leave us with a paradoxical image: a wedding altar that is also a chessboard, where vows are made in the language of strategy and hearts are often the first casualties. And if there's one thing that's clear, it's that while these unions might have worn the guise of marital "love," the real romance was always between power and opportunity.

Chapter 3

Royal Betrayals –
When Love Turns Lethal

Istory's love stories aren't all hearts and flowers – sometimes they're more like episodes of a true-crime podcast co-written by Shakespeare and *Game of Thrones*. In this chapter, we'll take a conversational stroll through three infamous royal relationship fiascos where "till death do us part" was taken way too literally. Grab your popcorn (and maybe a suit of armor), because these regal romances gone wrong have more drama than a Kardashian family dinner and more betrayal than a Taylor Swift breakup anthem.

We'll visit:

- Tudor England for the tumultuous saga of Henry VIII and Anne Boleyn, a power couple whose love story went from *head over heels* to just heads will roll.
- Imperial Russia to witness Catherine the Great and Peter III, where a marriage made in political heaven became a coup d'état with the bride on top – imagine a *Real Housewives* season finale, but with more Cossacks.
- Ancient Rome for the wild tale of Emperor Commodus, proving that *family therapy* might have saved the empire a lot of poison and paranoia.

Through these stories, we'll see how paranoia, power-lust, and manipulation turned cozy royal pillow talk into Machiavellian mayhem. And don't worry – we'll keep it humorous. After all, if we don't laugh at the absurdity of these historical soap operas, we might just cry (or lose our heads).

Henry VIII and Anne Boleyn: Tudor Tinder Gone Terribly Wrong

Henry VIII is basically the poster child for *"It's not you, it's me – and my kingdom needs an heir."* In the 1530s, King Henry of England was like a man in midlife crisis mode, but instead of buying a sports car, he founded his own church just to dump his wife and marry his new crush. Seriously – Henry broke England away from the Catholic Church so he could legally ditch Queen Catherine of Aragon and wed Anne Boleyn, all because he was obsessed with having a male heir. Talk about extreme relationship goals! It's as if Henry swiped right on Anne and then bribe… I mean *convinced* an entire nation's clergy to approve the match.

Anne Boleyn wasn't just some random court beauty; she was the *Marvel* superhero version of a Tudor lady – bold, clever, and totally determined to be Queen rather than mistress. She refused to be Henry's side-chick (her sister Mary Boleyn had already filled that role), insisting on a wedding ring instead. Henry was so smitten he wrote love letters and waited years to bed her – a bit like a Taylor Swift slow-burn romance.

But once Anne was queen, the honeymoon phase lasted about as long as a TikTok trend. She gave birth to a daughter (the future Elizabeth I), and Henry, expecting a boy, reacted as if she'd handed him a pair of socks for Christmas. Not exactly #DadOfTheYear. Anne tried – she suffered several miscarriages in her quest to produce a Tudor male heir – but by 1536 Henry's wandering eye had already landed on Jane Seymour. Suddenly Anne went from object of desire to royal inconvenience.

Now, if Henry had modern breakup tools, he might've just ghosted Anne or sent a "sorry, it's over" text. Instead, he went old-school: accusing her of heinous crimes to justify getting rid of her. (Ever heard of "treasonous adultery"? No? Henry basically invented it for the occasion.) In a plot twist no one saw coming – except maybe those who helped cook it up – Anne was charged with cheating on the King with not one, not two, but five men, including her own brother! Yes, you read that right. The Tudors essentially launched a Jerry Springer episode in court, complete with allegations of *incest*. It was the 16th-century equivalent of a tabloid scandal, only with far sharper consequences. Anne, of course, denied everything. Historians now agree the charges were about as solid as a house of cards in a hurricane – basically trumped-up nonsense so Henry could *legally* do what he wanted anyway.

A famously imposing portrait of King Henry VIII. His expression says, "I'm in charge," and indeed he was – even in his love life, where his solution to marital discord was often, well, final. This Tudor king collected wives like Thanos collecting Infinity Stones – except when he snapped his fingers, *heads* rolled.

Henry had Anne hauled off to the Tower of London, and in May 1536, after a show-trial, she was found guilty. Of course, she was – who was going to tell King Henry "no"? And so, in a move that officially ended their love story (and Anne's *entire* story), Henry ordered her execution. On a sunny morning (because fate has a cruel sense of humor), Anne Boleyn was beheaded by a skilled swordsman – an imported French executioner, since Henry at least had the decency to make it quick and relatively clean.

Let's pause to appreciate the absurdity here: Henry's idea of a breakup was capital punishment. That's like responding to a disappointing text from your partner by calling in the Avengers – complete overkill. Yet in Henry's mind, this was totally justified. He was paranoid that Anne's alleged infidelities made him look like a fool, and more importantly, her failure to produce a son threatened the Tudor dynasty.

Paranoia and power-lust danced a deadly tango: Henry *needed* to control his legacy, and if that meant eliminating a once-beloved wife, so be it. Love? Passion? Those were nice for the Instagram posts (or the Tudor equivalent, lavish love poems), but the real driver was control – controlling the succession, controlling the narrative (Henry's propaganda machine worked overtime to paint Anne as a witchy seductress), and controlling his own image as a *macho* king who wouldn't be played for a chump.

In the aftermath, Henry ultimately had six wives – the rhyme "divorced, beheaded, died; divorced, beheaded, survived" sums up that track record. Anne Boleyn, tragically, was the first of the beheaded. Henry clearly learned nothing about balancing love and power, as he continued putting his dynastic goals above any semblance of spousal loyalty.

Henry and Anne's story teaches us one thing: in the game of love vs. power, Henry always bet on power. When passion didn't serve his ambitions, he cut his losses – and his wife's head – to regain control. It's a grisly lesson wrapped in royal glamour. Through a darkly comic lens, we might say Henry VIII is that guy who "has no chill" when it comes to breakups. Instead of sending an apology or writing a sad love song, he literally rewrote his kingdom's religion and let the executioner handle his *relationship issues*. Talk about a toxic ex!

Catherine the Great and Peter III: A Marriage Coup d'État

If Henry and Anne were a tragic romance, Catherine the Great and Tsar Peter III were a dark comedy – think *Mr. & Mrs. Smith* but in imperial Russia, where Mrs. Smith stages a military coup against Mr. Smith and ends up *running* the whole show. #PowerCoupleGoals? Not exactly. More like #PowerStruggleGoals.

Picture this: It's 18th-century Russia, and Princess Sophie of Anhalt-Zerbst, later known as Catherine, marries the future Tsar Peter III. It's an arranged marriage – young Catherine is brought to Russia mainly to produce heirs and be a decorative consort. But Catherine isn't about to play trophy wife. While Peter spends his free time obsessively drilling his toy soldiers (rumor has it he even took toy figurines to bed), Catherine is hitting the books, reading Voltaire and learning to charm the Russian court. In essence, Catherine is training herself to rule, while Peter is busy playing pretend war.

When Peter finally became Tsar in 1762, he proved disastrously ill-suited to the job. The new emperor quickly angered crucial allies – from the powerful Orthodox Church to his own military – with tone-deaf policies. For instance, he made peace with Prussia (Russia's recent enemy) simply because he idolized King Frederick the Great, and he started sidelining Russian traditions in favor of Prussian drills and uniforms.

It's as if the CEO of a company suddenly started praising their arch-rival and undoing the team's big project – a surefire way to get ousted by the board. In this case, Catherine decided she *was* the board and her hapless husband was about to be voted off the island.

Enter Grigory Orlov, one of Catherine's lovers (scandalous!). Catherine wasn't exactly lonely during her unhappy marriage – let's just say she found companionship elsewhere. Orlov and his brothers happened to command a regiment of soldiers, which was awfully convenient. In July 1762, while Peter was off at a country estate doing who-knows-what (hopefully not still playing with his toy army), Catherine made her move. With the Orlovs' help, she rallied around 14,000 troops and marched on the capital to unseat her husband.

Catherine even put on a male guardsman's uniform and personally led the charge – a badass move that announced, *"I'm in charge now."* Peter, deserted by his own guards, basically said "ok, cool" and abdicated without much of a fight. At first the coup was almost bloodless; Catherine strolled into power with hardly a scuffle. She emerged from the Winter Palace as Empress of Russia, greeted by cheers (and probably a few stunned looks from courtiers picking their jaws off the floor).

Of course, a deposed ex-husband hanging around is a liability – especially when he's an ex-tsar with a claim to your throne. So, a few days after the coup, Peter III turned up dead while in custody. Officially, he perished in a "scuffle" with his guards. Unofficially, everyone pretty much assumed that Catherine's associates *arranged* his untimely demise. (The likely culprit was Alexei Orlov, Grigory's brother, who was conveniently guarding Peter and may have found the perfect excuse for a little strangulation session.)

Catherine later feigned shock and sadness, as one does, but historians are skeptical. As one biographer put it, the exact details will never be known – but let's be real, Catherine *greatly* benefited from Peter's abrupt exit.

A regal portrait of Empress Catherine II. She might look composed and sweet, but don't be fooled – behind those kind eyes was a master strategist who could give Kris Jenner a run for her money in the power-play department. Catherine understood that in the high-stakes game of ruling, power always trumped passion. Her marriage to Peter had been loveless from the start; once the chance to grab the throne appeared, any wifely affection was tossed aside like last season's court fashion.

Jokes aside, the lesson in this lethal love story is that Catherine and Peter's union was never about genuine passion. It was a cold transaction from the start – a political arrangement. When Peter became more useful to her as a casualty than as a husband, Catherine did not hesitate. Paranoia also played its part: she knew if *she* didn't remove Peter, he could be used by her enemies to remove *her*. So, she struck first. In a darkly comic sense, Catherine basically read The 48 Laws of Power instead of any fairy-tale marriage manual.

Catherine would go on to reign for 34 years as "the Great," one of Russia's most successful (and scandal-prone) rulers. But the grim irony behind that grand title is that she secured it through betraying her own spouse. Her hunger for control outweighed any shred of marital loyalty – a pattern we're seeing across these royal tales.

Emperor Commodus and the Toxic Family Feud

For our final tale, we journey to ancient Rome – where family drama was practically an Olympic sport (or maybe a gladiatorial match). If you thought your family gatherings were awkward, Emperor Commodus would like a word. His reign (180–192 AD) was a wild brew of paranoia and megalomania – a mashup of a supervillain origin story and *Keeping Up with the Kardashians* (but with more togas and way more stabbing). Commodus shows how paranoia and power-lust can turn a family bond into a ticking time bomb.

First, who was Commodus? He was the son of the wise Emperor Marcus Aurelius, but Commodus proved that the apple can fall very far from the tree. While his philosopher-king dad was all about duty and Stoic virtue, Commodus was all about *Commodus*. He literally renamed all the months of the year after himself – an act of vanity for the history books. He fancied himself a reincarnation of Hercules and had statues made depicting him in a lion-skin and wielding a club. Talk about a god complex.

Commodus even fought in the arena as a gladiator (naturally, he claimed victory in every rigged match). The Roman Senate and many citizens were horrified that the emperor would stoop so low, but Commodus *loved* the gladiatorial spotlight. Not surprisingly, the ruling class started thinking their emperor had lost his marbles – and they weren't wrong.

By 182 AD, the imperial family feud hit a new low: Commodus's own sister Lucilla engineered a plot to assassinate him. The attempt failed and Lucilla was exiled, then executed soon after. (When your big sister wants you dead, you *know* Thanksgiving is cancelled.) After that close call, Commodus descended into full-blown paranoia, executing anyone who even *looked* at him funny. He once had a servant tossed into an oven because his bath was lukewarm – yes, really. The message was clear: cross Commodus, and you're dead.

By late 192, Commodus drew up a list of people he intended to execute – and lo and behold, on it were his mistress Marcia, his top general (Laetus), and his chamberlain (Eclectus). When Marcia discovered her own name on this hit list, she and the others decided to get him before he got them. On December 31, 192, they served Commodus some *special* wine. He drank the poison and promptly vomited it back up (perhaps years of heavy partying gave him a strong stomach). Plan B: send in the wrestler. Commodus's personal trainer – a hulking fellow named Narcissus – was summoned, and he strangled the emperor in his bath. And just like that, Commodus's wild ride was over, courtesy of the people closest to him.

Marble bust of Emperor Commodus posed as Hercules. It's a fitting image for a man who thought he was a living god. Unfortunately for him, his loved ones didn't share that view. In the toxic atmosphere Commodus created, even those who supposedly cared for him felt compelled to betray him to save themselves. It became a classic Roman family free-for-all – essentially a real-life version of HBO's *Succession*, but with actual bloodshed. Trust and affection in Commodus's household? Long gone. Love had left the building once paranoia moved in, and everyone was out for themselves.

Commodus's grisly end shows how utterly fear and power-lust can poison family ties. His sister turned on him from jealousy and self-preservation. His mistress and friends turned on him because they knew he was about to do the same to them. Genuine love or loyalty didn't stand a chance in that lethal arena.

Conclusion: Love, Lust, and Power – A Not-So-Fairy-Tale

So, what do these royal trainwrecks tell us? There's a clear theme: when passion and paranoia mix in palace halls, power usually wins out over love. Through our (admittedly sarcastic) journey from Tudor England to Imperial Russia to ancient Rome, we've seen that these betrayals weren't crimes of passion in the heat of the moment – they were calculated moves in the chess game of power.

Let's recap with a few tongue-in-cheek life lessons gleaned from our deadly love stories:

- Keep the Axe out of Arguments: If your royal spouse starts sharpening a sword during a marital spat, that's a red flag. (Henry VIII, we're looking at you – maybe try counseling instead of execution.)

- Never Underestimate the Quiet One: That seemingly demure spouse might be plotting your overthrow. (Just ask Peter III – Catherine played the long game.)

- Don't Put Your Lover on a Hit List: If you plan to murder your closest allies, don't be surprised if they try to murder you first. Commodus learned this the hard way.

- Power is the Ultimate Aphrodisiac – and Poison: These monarchs loved power even more than their partners. When love and power conflicted, power won every time – with deadly results.

Ultimately, each of these lethal love stories came down to one thing: the hunger for power overshadowing any genuine affection. Henry wasn't heartbroken – he was safeguarding his ego and dynasty. Catherine's coup wasn't about lost love – it was a cold-blooded career move. Commodus's inner circle didn't betray him over petty family drama – they struck out of fear for their lives.

So, the next time you witness a messy celebrity breakup or a political power couple's feud, remember these royal cautionary tales. At least today a bad split usually means a few bitter tweets or a hit breakup song – not a scaffold or a poisoned chalice. And if there's one more lesson: never date a monarch. It's hazardous to your health!

Chapter 4

Scandal and Sensation –
Royals Who Shocked Their Worlds

Royal scandals are the original reality show: centuries before Netflix and TMZ, monarchs were out here living wild lives that left their kingdoms clutching their pearls. We tend to picture royalty as buttoned-up figures waving politely from balconies – but surprise! Some royals break the rules so flamboyantly they make today's celebrity scandals look tame. In this chapter, we'll dish on three historical royals who truly *shocked their worlds*: a British princess whose love life sparked a constitutional crisis, a Bavarian king so eccentric he made fairy tale castles (and possibly a few boyfriends on the side), and a Madagascan queen whose idea of "date night" sometimes involved an execution order. Buckle up your crown jewels; it's about to get irreverent.

We're diving into stories of public scandal, personal rebellion, and epic clashes with tradition. But don't worry – we'll serve it with a wink and plenty of modern analogies. Think of it as history told by a stand-up comic who raided the royal archives. From a princess who wanted to marry Mr. Wrong (but Mr. So Right), to a king whose best relationship was with a castle, to a queen who put the "dead" in deadly romance, these tales blend the outrageous truth with a satirical twist.

Scandal and sensation, indeed – even Shonda Rhimes couldn't make this stuff up.

Princess Margaret and Peter Townsend – The Princess and the Divorcé

Once upon a time in stiff-upper-lip 1950s Britain, Princess Margaret rose each morning, polished her tiara, and *perhaps* hummed "I Wanna Be Loved by You" under her breath. Margaret was Queen Elizabeth II's kid sister – the royal spare with flair, a party girl with a razor-sharp wit. She was the human embodiment of a cheeky gin and tonic: fun, a bit strong, and liable to leave the establishment with a hangover. So naturally, when it came to love, Margaret didn't fall for some bland aristocrat. Nope. Our princess set her sights on Captain Peter Townsend – a dashingly handsome World War II fighter pilot, commoner servant of the royal household, and (scandal of scandals) a divorcé 16 years her senior. If this were a Disney movie, the princess would have eloped and lived happily ever after. But this was the House of Windsor, and in 1953 that meant *no happy endings with divorced dudes allowed.*

Let's paint the scene: Margaret, in her early 20s, was sparkling at palace parties and probably sneaking cigarettes behind the throne. Enter Peter Townsend, the King's equerry (basically a glorified gopher with a uniform) and certified war hero. He was older, experienced, and – oh yes – freshly divorced from his unfaithful wife. In the fairy tale version, the dashing pilot rescues the princess from her tower. In the royal reality version, the dashing pilot flirted with the princess by helping her climb *into* a tower (he allegedly boosted her into a window when she forgot the key once – true story). It wasn't long before Margaret was head over heels, and Townsend was equally smitten by the fun-loving princess. He later gushed that Margaret had *"a girl-of-the-year figure and a raucous laugh that made you bend double,"* or something to that effect. This was no mere fling – the two were very much in love, making goo-goo eyes at each other in corridors of Buckingham Palace while trying to dodge prying butler eyes.

Now, you might ask: what's the big deal? Today, royal marrying a divorced person is practically chic (hi, Charles and Camilla!). But back then, this romance was the equivalent of Harry falling for a Hollywood actress – *oh wait*, that happened – well, worse, actually. Marrying a divorcé was forbidden by the Church of England, the very church Margaret's sister headed. The last time a royal tried to marry a divorced person, King Edward VIII literally quit his job (abdicated the throne in 1936) to do it. The Royal Family wasn't exactly eager for a sequel to that fiasco. So poor Queen Elizabeth II, barely settled on the throne, was presented with a nightmare: her own sister was asking permission to marry a man that half the country (the fun half) cheered for, and the other half (the stuffy half in Parliament and the Church) absolutely *loathed* the idea of. At the tender age of 25, Elizabeth had to play referee between true love and royal duty – which, incidentally, would make a great tagline for a soap opera.

The public got wind of the secret love in the most adorably British way imaginable. During Elizabeth's grand coronation in 1953, sharp-eyed reporters caught Princess Margaret in a *truly scandalous act* – she picked a bit of lint off Peter Townsend's uniform. Yes, that's right. One stray piece of fluff, removed ever-so-tenderly, and the tabloids lost their collective minds. In 1950s Britain, you might as well have caught them snogging in Westminster Abbey; a princess *touching* a man's jacket was basically second base in those days. The press printed the fluff-flinging incident worldwide, and suddenly "Margaret ♥ Peter" was the hottest news, prompting eyebrow raises from London to Timbuktu. Never underestimate the erotic power of a lint-brush moment.

As public excitement grew – most regular Brits were rooting for this real-life Cinderella story – the Establishment dug in its heels. Margaret was *under 25*, which by law meant she needed the Queen's formal consent to marry. More awkwardly, as monarch and Head of the Church, big sis Elizabeth was expected to say, "Over my dead corgi!" to any union with a divorced man. The government wasn't any cooler about it either. Prime Minister Winston Churchill (hardly a progressive on matters of the heart) indicated his Cabinet would resign rather than approve this marriage. Imagine: the *entire government* ready to quit just because the Princess might tie the knot with her dream guy. Talk about high stakes for a relationship – it's like threatening to cancel the Super Bowl because the quarterback might marry a Kardashian.

The royal solution? Banish the handsome pilot! Poor Peter Townsend got promptly shipped off to Brussels on a diplomatic posting – the classic "let's send the naughty lovebirds far, far away" maneuver. (One can only picture Peter in Belgium, sadly kicking cobblestones and wondering if Belgian beer could cure heartache.) For two years Margaret and Peter carried on a long-distance romance via love letters and furtive meetups. The British press kept gossiping; the people kept swooning. Polls at the time showed a majority of the public actually *supported* Margaret marrying Townsend – a rare instance of commoners rooting for a royal to marry a commoner, rather than some inbred continental princeling. It was a full-blown media circus: think Team Margaret vs Team Duty on every newspaper, debated at pubs over pints of ale.

Then came 1955, the year of decision. Margaret turned 25, finally old enough to tell her sister "I don't need your permission, I can marry who I want!". *Technically*, by hitting that magic birthday, she gained the legal right to choose her spouse. *But*, (there's always a but), the Establishment still wasn't backing down. In fact, they pulled a sneaky maneuver: Parliament offered to tweak the rules so she could marry Townsend – *if* she agreed to give up her royal status, income, home, basically everything short of her fabulous jewelry collection. In other words, "Sure, go ahead and marry for love… just stop being a princess and please close the door on your way out of the palace." Talk about a poisoned chalice – the choice was true love in exile or a crown with an asterisk ("no fun allowed").

For a hot minute, it looked like Margaret might actually do it. Love conquers all, right? Well, love *almost* conquered Margaret's love of being a royal. She and Peter reunited in '55 for a face-to-face talk, and one imagines the conversation went like this: *Peter:* "Darling, run away with me, we'll grow roses in Brussels!" *Margaret:* "Umm, do they even have high society in Brussels? Also, I rather fancy being Her Royal Highness…" It was an impossible dilemma. In a final gut-wrenching decision, Margaret chose the crown over her heart. On October 31, 1955 – Halloween, of all fitting days – she publicly announced she would *not* marry Peter Townsend. In her official statement (crafted with all the emotional transparency of a brick wall), she said she had decided to put "the Church's teachings" and her "duty to the Commonwealth" above "any others". In plain English: *God and country told me not to, so I'm dumping my boyfriend. Ouch.* Britain collectively wept into its tea. It was the royal equivalent of canceling the finale of a beloved TV romance – *heartbreaking*, but oh-so-civilized on the surface.

Princess Margaret's love life didn't exactly become sunshine and rainbows after that. She was reportedly heartbroken, chain-smoking through her sorrows (the woman loved her cigarettes almost as much as she'd loved Peter). But being Margaret, she wasn't about to join a convent. She later married society photographer Antony Armstrong-Jones (a.k.a. Lord Snowdon) in 1960 – a match that started out as a swinging-'60s fairy tale and ended in a 1978 divorce amid tales of wild parties and extra-marital shenanigans (Margaret *knew* how to keep the tabloids happy). As for Peter Townsend, our jilted pilot didn't stay single forever. He moved to France and, in a plot twist nobody scripted, married a young woman who looked *shockingly* like a Princess Margaret doppelgänger. (Apparently, the man had a type – and if he couldn't have the real Maggie, a look-alike would do. Freud would have a field day with that one.) The two former lovebirds did meet one last time in the 1990s, as old friends with a wistful shared past. When Margaret died in 2002, the world remembered her as the *royal rebel* who almost upended the monarchy for love. In hindsight, her story feels like an ultra-posh rom-com that turned into a tragedy because the heroine wouldn't elope. It had all the ingredients: forbidden love, public scandal, noble self-sacrifice – basically "The Crown" with a punchier script. Margaret's romance with Townsend showed that even a princess couldn't have it all. But boy, did she give the Establishment a royal migraine while it lasted.

In the end, Princess Margaret did what so many of us do – she *moved on.* But not before leaving an indelible mark on the royal family's image. She was the original "people's princess" in that the people actually sided with *her* against the stuffy government. She also set the stage for future royal rule-breakers. Imagine being a young Prince Harry, hearing Great-Auntie Margaret's saga at tea time – you'd be taking notes for your own grand escape later. The clash between Margaret's personal rebellion and royal tradition was a real doozy: a public scandal that had the monarchy *this close* to modernizing decades earlier than it actually did. And through it all, Margaret kept her chin up, her humor intact, and likely a cocktail in hand. As a wise (fictional) princess once sang, "Let it go." Margaret did – and the ripples from her forbidden love story still fascinate us today.

King Ludwig II of Bavaria – The Mad King's Fairy-Tale Romances

If Princess Margaret's scandal was all stiff British upper lips quivering, King Ludwig II of Bavaria's life was more like an absurdist opera – fitting since the man was obsessed with operas. In fact, Ludwig's story has everything: beautiful castles, mystery, possible insanity, and enough eccentric romance to fuel a dozen tabloid covers (or at least a really juicy season of Bridgerton set in the 19th century). Picture a tall, dreamy-eyed king who'd rather daydream and design fantasy castles than, you know, govern a country. That's Ludwig in a nutshell. He's often nicknamed "Mad King Ludwig," but honestly, "Fabulously Weird King Ludwig" might be more accurate. His worlds of love and fantasy were so intertwined that Bavaria ended up with architectural fever dreams, and Ludwig's ministers ended up with ulcers.

Ludwig became King of Bavaria in 1864 at just 18 – basically a teenager with a crown, *never a good combo.* He inherited a kingdom needing real leadership, but Ludwig said "Nah, I'm going to build literal fairy-tale castles and fanboy over my favorite composer instead." His idea of kingly duty was funding the arts and taking midnight sleigh rides through the Alps dressed in historical costumes (yes, he did that). The greatest love of Ludwig's life arguably wasn't a person at all – it was music. Specifically, the operatic epics of Richard Wagner. Ludwig *loved* Wagner's music like it was the Beyoncé of his day. When he wasn't gazing longingly at swans (his spirit animal) or sketching turret designs, Ludwig was writing gushing letters to Wagner and sponsoring the composer's wild creative ambitions. Some folks whispered that Ludwig's passion for Wagner wasn't *just* about music. Rumors flew around Munich that the young king had a bit of a crush on the older composer – an infatuation that *might* have gone beyond patronage into the territory of "unrequited love affair with dramatic musical soundtrack." We'll never know for sure, but Ludwig's letters to Wagner were about as subtle as a tuba solo. In one letter he basically places himself "in [Wagner's] angelic arms" – you can practically see the heart emojis. Wagner, for his part, was happy to encourage the king's *ahem* affection – after all, Ludwig's wallet was funding his operas. This may be the only time in history that a composer was essentially a king's long-distance crush *and* sugar baby.

While Wagner was Ludwig's artistic soulmate, there were flesh-and-blood romances (or attempted romances) in the king's life too – though none ended in a traditional happily ever after. Ludwig was *engaged* once, believe it or not. Pressured to produce an heir (kings gotta king), he got betrothed in 1867 to his own cousin, Duchess

60

Sophie of Bavaria. Sophie was beautiful, cultured, and conveniently came from the family – what could go wrong? Well, for starters, Ludwig showed more passion for the works of Wagner that he and Sophie both adored than for Sophie herself. It's as if the only thing holding their engagement together was their mutual love for the opera *Lohengrin*. (In fact, Ludwig's letters to Sophie read like a Wagner fan club newsletter – he literally wrote that their relationship was based on "Richard Wagner's remarkable destiny". Talk about *romantic* pillow talk!) Wedding planning proceeded in a half-hearted way, with Ludwig dragging his heels. He postponed the wedding date *again and again*, finding any excuse – "Sorry, can't get married yet, I'm *this* close to finishing design on my fantasy castle, priorities!" – until finally he just *cancelled* the whole shebang. Cold feet doesn't begin to cover it. To pour salt on the wound (or maybe to give it a dramatic flourish), Ludwig sent Sophie a breakup letter referencing characters from Wagner's opera: he addressed her as "Elsa" and himself as "Heinrich," lamenting that her cruel father (like an opera villain) tore them apart. Yes, he basically ghosted his fiancée via cosplay letter. Imagine being Sophie: you've been dumped *in character*. The 19th century had its own version of being broken up with by someone who quotes sad song lyrics at you. Unsurprisingly, Sophie moved on (marrying someone else), and Ludwig showed up unexpectedly at her wedding reception – because why not make it more awkward?

So, Ludwig never married. In fact, after Sophie, he never even *pretended* to chase eligible princesses. Instead, he poured all that romantic energy into his fantasy projects and close friendships. How close, you ask? Well, Ludwig's diaries and private letters (uncovered later) reveal that he struggled with being gay or bisexual in a very conservative time. He was a devout Catholic, and while Bavaria had decriminalized homosexuality briefly, the newly unified Germany brought back harsh laws against it in 1871. So, Ludwig lived a double life: public celibacy, private yearning. He kept a string of extremely handsome male companions at court – his aide-de-camp Prince Paul von Thurn und Taxis, his chief equerry (a fancy term for "guy who helps the king with horses") Richard Hornig, a good-looking actor named Josef Kainz, and more. The palace gossip mill definitely buzzed. One official even acted as Ludwig's *personal matchmaker/procurer* for attractive young men. (There's a job title you won't see on LinkedIn: Royal Procurer of Hunks, 1860s edition.) These relationships were mostly discreet, but you can imagine the shockwaves if the Bavarian public had known their dreamy monarch wasn't exactly pining for princesses.

For Ludwig, romance and fantasy blended in spectacular fashion. While other kings went to war or passed laws, Ludwig built castles – and *boy* did he build. His most famous creation, Neuschwanstein Castle, looks like it sprang from a child's fairy-tale book or perhaps an acid trip involving Cinderella. (Disney fans, take note: Neuschwanstein *literally* inspired the iconic Sleeping Beauty Castle design – meaning this Bavarian king indirectly gave us the backdrop for countless Disney films. Not bad for a so-called madman!). ** *Neuschwanstein Castle, one of Ludwig II's extravagant creations – essentially a gigantic love letter to fantasy and Wagnerian opera. It later inspired Disneyland's Sleeping Beauty Castle, proving that Ludwig was living in a fairy tale of his own making.* ** In Ludwig's mind, each castle was a stage for the grand romance he imagined life should be. Neuschwanstein, for instance, was dedicated to Wagner's operas – each room a shrine to scenes from *Tristan and Isolde* or *Lohengrin*, tales of star-crossed lovers and mystical swans. It's as if he said, "Who needs a queen when I have a perfectly good castle to cuddle with?" He also built Linderhof Palace (a cozy little luxury villa where he dined alone at a table set for Louis XIV – yes, he ate imaginary dinners with the long-dead French Sun King, which might be taking fanboying a tad far) and Herrenchiemsee, a partial replica of Versailles complete with a Hall of Mirrors. Ludwig essentially role-played as his idol Louis XIV of France, minus the actual political power. Imagine someone today building their own White House replica to LARP as the President – that's the level of extra we're dealing with.

As Ludwig sank deeper into his fantasy world, his government grew frustrated. The king's romances – whether with castles or courtiers – were draining the treasury and producing zero heirs. The Bavarian ministers were like, "Is he *ever* coming out of that swan-shaped boat to do some governing?" By the 1880s, Ludwig's behavior (midnight sleigh rides, isolating in his castles by day, summoning servants for theatre-like productions at odd hours) convinced his ministers that he'd truly lost his marbles. In 1886, they executed a coup of sorts: they had Ludwig declared insane and deposed. Now, was he actually insane? Debatable. Perhaps he was just eccentric and introverted, a romantic dreamer ill-suited to realpolitik. But the fact remains, they carted him off like a patient, not a king. In a mysterious and grim epilogue, Ludwig died just days after being removed from the throne – found dead in a shallow lake alongside the very psychiatrist who had certified him insane. (Sounds like the setup to an Agatha Christie novel, doesn't it? Officially, Ludwig's death was ruled a suicide by drowning, but suspiciously no water was found in his lungs. Meanwhile, the psychiatrist had blows to the head. Conspiracy theories abound: Was it murder? An escape attempt gone wrong? One theory even has Ludwig shot by his enemies while trying to flee. In Bavaria, folks still debate "Who killed the King?" over their beer steins. It's the royal scandal that keeps on giving.)

King Ludwig II's legacy is complex. He shocked his world not with one big scandalous affair, but with a lifetime of *extraordinary* defiance of norms. He defied what a king was supposed to be – he played the lover, the patron, the dreamer, more than the ruler. He rebelled against the boring reality of monarchy by transforming Bavaria into a backdrop for his personal theater of dreams. The public at the time was equal parts horrified and fascinated by their "mad" king. Nowadays, Bavaria profits nicely from Ludwig's madness – those castles bring in millions of tourist dollars. (Irony alert: the king who bankrupted his treasury for love of art is now the region's biggest cash cow.) In a modern lens, Ludwig might be seen as a tragic romantic figure, perhaps a man born in the wrong century. He was *too* dreamy for the real world, a sensitive soul who tried to make life as beautiful as the operas he adored. His clash with tradition – spurning a dynastic marriage, neglecting statecraft for personal passions – ended in tragedy, but left behind literal monuments to imagination. And though his love life remained unfulfilled in the conventional sense, Ludwig's story has its own strange romance: a king in love with beauty itself, unwilling to settle for the ordinary. In a way, he gave his kingdom not an heir, but something arguably more fabulous – enchantment, mystery, and a scandal that still echoes like Wagner's lingering notes.

Queen Ranavalona I of Madagascar – The Queen of Mean and Her Lover Troubles

Hold onto your heads (literally) for this one, because Queen Ranavalona I of Madagascar makes other scandalous royals look like kittens. If Princess Margaret's tale was a romantic drama and Ludwig's was a gothic opera, Ranavalona's story is a blood-soaked action thriller with a dark comic streak. This 19th-century queen ruled Madagascar from 1828 to 1861, and her idea of "clashing with tradition" was to grab tradition by the throat and force-feed it poison. She has been dubbed "the Female Caligula", "the Mad Queen of Madagascar," and other choice nicknames that basically imply you wouldn't want to meet her in a dark alley – or in a well-lit throne room, for that matter. But beneath the tales of gore lies a story of a woman who *refused* to bow to anyone – not to foreign powers, not to new religions, and certainly not to any man who thought he could tame her. And she did it all while juggling a *very* spicy love life that would make a soap opera writer blush.

Ranavalona didn't start out as a bloodthirsty monarch (no one comes out of the womb yelling "Off with their heads!"). Born around 1778 and originally named Ramavo, she married Prince Radama – heir to the King of Madagascar – thanks to a twist of fate where her dad foiled a plot against the king. You could say she got married by royal command – a kind of "thanks for saving my life, here's my son's hand in marriage" reward. Not exactly *The Bachelor*, but it got her a ring. Young Ramavo became one of King Radama I's many wives (polygamy was normal in Malagasy culture). Unfortunately, Radama wasn't exactly a loving hubby. In fact, history suggests he straight-up ignored Ranavalona for years. They had zero children in two decades of marriage – a fact that probably had the royal gossip mill churning, because producing heirs was *the* job of a chief wife. Rumor has it they hated each other's guts (20 years of bickering and no babies – sounds loveless enough). So, when Radama died in 1828, Ranavalona likely felt *zero* grief and 100% determination. Through some adept palace politicking (read: likely eliminating a few rivals, as one does), she seized power for herself and became queen.

Here's where things go from 0 to 100 on the scandal-o-meter. Queen Ranavalona I decided Madagascar needed a hardcore rewind to tradition. Her late hubby had been chummy with the British and even let missionaries in to spread Christianity. Ranavalona said, "Nah, not on my watch." She essentially declared war on European influence – not a polite diplomatic pushback, but a violent purge. Missionaries? Persecuted or kicked out. Converts to Christianity? Hunted down and subjected to something called the tangena ordeal. Now, brace yourself for this: the tangena ordeal was a trial by poison. Suspected Christians (or other "traitors" in her eyes) were forced to eat a poisonous nut and some chicken skin, then vomit. If three pieces of skin came up, congratulations, you're innocent! If not – well, you probably died from the poison or got speared on the spot. *That* was Ranavalona's justice system. She basically said, "My kingdom, my rules – and my rules are *terrifying.*" The result? Madagascar's population literally halved under her 33-year reign (from around 5 million to 2.5 million) due to executions, forced labor, disease, and constant warfare. Let that sink in: up to 50% of her people perished during her rule. We're talking possibly millions dead – making her one of history's deadliest monarchs by percentage. Eat your heart out, *Game of Thrones*. This queen piled up a body count that would make HBO execs say "too unrealistic!"

Amidst all this tyrannical terror, Ranavalona had *needs*, you know? She was a widow in her prime and clearly not the shy, retiring type. Enter the lovers. Her love life post-Radama was, as one historian delicately put it, "messy." Translation: the royal bedchamber had a revolving door (and probably a trapdoor for those who displeased her). First up was a dashing military officer named Andrianamihaja – we'll call him "Andy" for brevity. Andy was handsome, brave, and conveniently helped Ranavalona secure the throne. The two hooked up, and lo and behold, about a year after Radama's death, the Queen gave birth to a son, Prince Rakoto. Now, official records politely list Radama (the dead king) as the father – but c'mon, we can do the math. When a baby arrives 12 months after the king's death, let's just say *Radama had no part in that production*. It was an open secret that Prince Rakoto (later King Radama II) was *Andy's* son. So Ranavalona was already shattering protocol: a queen with a "bastard" heir by a lover? Oh, the scandal – at least to Europeans, who clutched their pearls so hard they turned to dust.

But wait, it gets juicier and darker. The love affair between Ranavalona and Andrianamihaja didn't end with cigars and champagne. Depending on who you ask, it ended with either murder or a drunken royal freak-out (or both). Version one: Ranavalona took a second lover, and that new guy *killed* Andy out of jealousy. Version two (the more tabloid-worthy one): Some conservative courtiers *hated* how much influence lover-boy Andy had, so they schemed to take him down. One night, they allegedly got the queen sloshed on palm wine and convinced her that Andrianamihaja was a traitor who used *witchcraft* to seduce her. (The old "he put a spell on you" trick – classic!) In her angry, inebriated state, Ranavalona signed his death warrant. Next thing you know, poor Andy was executed – reportedly speared to death while defending himself, if folk tales are to be believed. She basically executed her own baby-daddy. Talk about a toxic relationship. Forget blocking your ex's number; Ranavalona's breakup method was more like, "Off with his head." The French later described this saga with that colorful "Female Caligula" label, and honestly, it fits: lethal whims and lover drama were kind of her brand.

After Andrianamihaja's messy end, Ranavalona didn't exactly retire to a nunnery. She continued to take companions as she pleased. Notably, she formed a partnership (both political and probably personal) with a General Rainiharo, who became her Prime Minister. Rainiharo was fiercely loyal, helped run the kingdom, and conveniently kept the queen's bed warm for a while. He even got a tomb near hers eventually – a sign he was important to her. When Rainiharo passed away, Ranavalona, not one to stay single long, married another officer named Andrianisa (also called Rainijohary). This guy lasted till the end of her life, officially as her husband and PM. So, she *did* settle down… in her 70s… with Husband #2 (or #3, depending how you count). Essentially, the Queen of Mean had a series of leading men, and woe to any who fell out of favor. It's like a deadly season of "The Bachelorette," where losing the queen's rose might cost you your head.

While her love life provides ample gossip fodder, the scandals of Queen Ranavalona I go beyond the bedroom. She shocked her world by absolutely obliterating the norms of both her own culture (which had begun to open up under the previous king) and the expectations of the Western powers sniffing around Madagascar. She was a one-woman rebellion against colonial interference. Europeans called her savage and insane, mainly because she didn't give them trade concessions and literally shot at or decapitated those who tried to mess with her island. One French envoy's entire party got massacred on her orders when they attempted to impose a treaty. She even once supposedly declared war on mosquitoes – halting a French advance by having a swamp flooded to breed malarial mosquitoes that knocked out the invaders (clapback level: legendary). Her methods were brutal, but she was *successful* in one sense: during her reign, Madagascar *stayed independent.* She kept the British and French colonial wolves at bay for over 30 years. Of course, she also devastated her own population to do it, which is where that "insane tyrant" reputation comes in. Was she protecting her people's sovereignty, or just a sadistic tyrant? Probably a bit of both. Modern historians debate it, noting that the "evil queen" narrative was pushed by Europeans who were salty that she shut their influence down. But even if you give her credit as an anti-colonial resistor, you can't exactly excuse the *extreme* cruelty she employed. It's a bit like saying *Darth Vader* maintained order in the galaxy – true, but at what cost?

No description of Ranavalona is complete without some jaw-dropping anecdotes. She had a *flair* for the dramatic execution. Favorites included flinging enemies off cliffs into rocky ravines (with a troop at the bottom to finish off any survivors) and a personal twist on impalement where she'd have people's body parts crushed with steel implements. One possibly apocryphal story (but widely told because it's so horrific it sounds almost cartoonish) is that during one mass execution by fire, a woman gave birth as she was about to be burned. Ranavalona's soldiers promptly tossed the newborn *into the flames* – a ghastly tale mirrored in legends about other "bad queens" like England's Bloody Mary. Whether that specific event happened or not, it shows how her contemporaries viewed her: as a monster capable of anything. Yet here's an absurd twist – she was also known to throw opulent parties at her palace, complete with singing, dancing, and rivers of rum, which *also* contributed to that "Female Caligula" moniker. One minute she's hosting a grand ball, the next she's deciding which nobles to execute for dessert. It's like if Martha Stewart and Hannibal Lecter shared one body.

Amid all this, you have to admire a certain *dark sense of humor* in how Ranavalona viewed herself. She famously declared that as sovereign she was both man and woman, mother and father to her people. A practical move in a patriarchal world, sure, but also kind of a tongue-in-cheek *"I am the entire universe, deal with it"* statement. Way ahead of her time in the gender department – she basically said, "Call me King *and* Queen." It's as if she knew her reign was so outlandish, so against the norm, that she had to transcend gender just to justify it. In a modern comedy special, one can imagine her saying: *"I wear the pants and the skirt in this relationship!"*

Ranavalona I died peacefully in her bed at about 83 years old – which is wild considering how many people probably wished her a more... violent end. When she finally kicked the bucket in 1861, Madagascar practically breathed a sigh of relief. Her son Rakoto succeeded her as King Radama II and immediately tried to reverse mom's *kill-em-all* policies (only to be assassinated himself two years later – ruling that island was a tough gig). But get this: Ranavalona had such an impact that it took *decades* for Madagascar to really open up again. The French and British newspapers practically threw parties at the news of her death, painting her as this gothic villain finally vanquished. She remains a controversial figure: *was she the worst monarch ever, or a national hero for keeping Madagascar independent?* Perhaps both can be a little true. In any case, her story is the stuff of scandal legend.

Looking at Queen Ranavalona's life through a modern, irreverent lens, you almost have to laugh at the sheer absurdity and brutality of it. It's like Quentin Tarantino directed a historical epic and then The Onion wrote the subtitles. She defied every norm – a woman taking absolute power, snubbing imperial Europe, and treating lovers as disposable entertainment – and in doing so, shocked not just her world but the entire 19th-century colonial world watching. Her public scandals were on a grand geopolitical scale, and her personal rebellions (like executing cheating lovers or idiotic advisors) were the gossip of the age. This was a queen who literally put the *dead* in deadly romance. The lesson here might be: if you think your dating life is chaotic, be glad you're not a royal consort in 1850s Madagascar. And if you ever feel tyrannical bosses are bad, be glad you didn't work for Queen Ranavalona – she'd not only fire you, she might set you on fire.

From forbidden royal love to fairy-tale obsessions to murderous queens, these royals truly shocked their worlds. They thumbed their noses (and occasionally waved their swords) at tradition, creating scandals that left lasting marks on history. Yet, in their defiance, we find more than just salacious gossip – we see human stories of yearning and rebellion. Princess Margaret showed that even a gilded cage is still a cage when it comes to the heart's desires. King Ludwig II lived as if life could be as magical as art, scandalizing his ministers but leaving art lovers forever grateful. Queen Ranavalona I proved that a woman on the throne could be as formidable (or more so) than any man – and if the world didn't like it, the world could literally *drop dead.*

History tends to remember the prim and proper monarchs kindly, but it's the rule-breakers and rabble-rousers that make it truly interesting. They are the royal renegades who turned their palaces into stages for scandals and sensations. And let's be honest – we love them for it. After all, if you can't gossip about a queen executing her ex or a king building a fantasy castle for his crush, what's the point of history? These stories remind us that behind the titles and tiaras, royals are as imperfect, passionate, and peculiarly hilarious as the rest of us. In a world that expected them to conform, they said "heck no" in the most flamboyant ways possible. And centuries later, here we are, still chuckling, gasping, and raising our eyebrows at their exploits. Scandal and sensation, indeed – long may it reign.

Chapter 5

Tragic Love –
When Destiny Denied Happiness

Crown Prince Rudolf & Mary Vetsera – A Royal Romeo and Juliet at Mayerling

In the late 19th century, the Austro-Hungarian Empire witnessed a royal scandal with all the juicy elements of a soap opera – except it ended in literal tragedy. Crown Prince Rudolf, heir to the throne, fell in love with the young Baroness Mary Vetsera (pictured above in 1888) and their affair became the talk of Vienna. What happened next at the imperial hunting lodge of Mayerling in January 1889 was straight out of a gothic thriller: a murder–suicide pact that left both the 30-year-old prince and his 17-year-old lover dead, sending shockwaves through the royal family and beyond.

To set the stage, Rudolf was the only son of Emperor Franz Joseph and the famous Empress "Sisi" Elisabeth, which basically made him the *crown jewel* of the Habsburg dynasty (no pressure, right?). By all accounts, Rudolf was a smart guy but a tortured soul. He was stuck in a loveless arranged marriage with Princess Stéphanie of Belgium, chafing under an ultra-conservative father, and indulging in all sorts of vices to cope. (Picture a Victorian-era bad boy: reportedly depressed, anxious, and popping whatever passed for drugs in the 1880s.) His relationship with Mary Vetsera, a spirited 17-year-old baroness, was an open secret and a source of constant friction with Emperor Franz Joseph. Dad wanted Rudolf to dump the girlfriend, sober up, and focus on producing heirs; Rudolf wanted, well, *love* and maybe a bit of personal freedom. This was a classic generational clash—think *The Crown* meets rebellious teen drama, but with an imperial twist.

By late January 1889, Rudolf's mental state had hit rock-bottom. He and Mary retreated to Rudolf's hunting lodge at Mayerling, ostensibly for a romantic getaway or perhaps to plan an escape from their untenable reality. What unfolded there still fascinates (and haunts) historians. On the morning of January 30, both were found shot dead in the bedroom of the lodge. The official story: a double suicide out of hopeless love, a pact between two star-crossed lovers who felt their world would never accept them. In other words, Rudolf and Mary pulled a real-life Romeo and Juliet—if Romeo had been a depressed prince with a handgun and Juliet a teenage baroness with a fatal devotion.

Of course, the Habsburg court handled this about as well as you'd expect a 19th-century imperial family to handle scandal: with denial, cover-ups, and a frantic call to the Pope. (Rudolf was Catholic, so suicide was a big no-no—they initially tried to claim it was "natural causes" until that just didn't hold up.) Conspiracy theories blossomed like wildflowers. Whispers in Vienna wondered, *Was it an assassination? A politically motivated murder?* Some even alleged Emperor Franz Joseph might have had a hand in it (imagine suggesting a father would order a hit on his own son—that's how absurd and desperate the rumors got). But no credible evidence for foul play ever emerged. The simplest and most poignant explanation remains that Rudolf and Mary felt tragically cornered by destiny—unable to be together in life, they chose to unite in death. Dark, yes. Heartbreaking, absolutely.

The fallout was immense. Rudolf had been the heir apparent, so his death upended the imperial succession. The throne passed to Franz Joseph's brother and then to Archduke Franz Ferdinand—yep, the same Franz Ferdinand whose assassination in 1914 lit the fuse for World War I. It's chilling to think about: a personal tragedy at Mayerling set off a domino effect that eventually contributed to a global catastrophe. Talk about the butterfly effect, or rather the "Mayerling effect". On a more intimate level, Rudolf's mother, Empress Elisabeth, was devastated (she already had a morbid streak, and losing her only son plunged her deeper into sorrow), and the imperial family was cloaked in grief and embarrassment. Mary Vetsera's family, meanwhile, had to endure both the loss of their daughter and the insensitive gossip that follows a scandal. The whole empire was left reeling, as if a rug had been yanked from under the throne.

From a modern lens, it's hard not to imagine "what if." What if someone in Rudolf's circle had recognized his suicidal despair and intervened with compassion? What if the Emperor had been empathetic enough to let his son divorce and seek happiness, or at least listened to his grievances about the stifling court life? These are idle musings, but they highlight the moral undercurrent of the Mayerling tale. Rudolf was a man under immense generational pressure – the weight of centuries of tradition and expectation – and he crumbled. Instead of receiving help, he was essentially told to "man up" and carry on. Mary, barely out of girlhood, threw all her hope behind a prince who saw no way out. It's a recipe for disaster that no one chose to rewrite.

Historically, the Mayerling incident has become legendary – the subject of films, plays, even ballets (apparently, tragic death sells tickets). One commentator dubbed it "the late nineteenth-century equivalent of the Prince Charles and Lady Di affair" in terms of public fascination. In its day, it was a scandal for the ages, with every parlor in Europe buzzing about the doomed lovers. Today, we might compare it to a mashup of a royal tell-all memoir and a true-crime podcast. Except, behind the lurid details, there's a sobering lesson: unaddressed mental anguish + zero empathy + ironclad tradition = catastrophe. Rudolf and Mary's love was denied a place in life by forces they felt powerless to change – and so they chose to write a grim final chapter for themselves. In doing so, they inadvertently handed down a cautionary tale to posterity: even princes and baronesses can succumb to despair when happiness is barred by duty, and if nobody around them stops to care, the ending might just be tragically irreversible.

Princess Ka'iulani of Hawai'i – An Engagement Lost to a Kingdom Lost

Princess Ka'iulani was, in many ways, Hawai'i's own Cinderella – but one whose story got commandeered by a greedy fairy godfather called colonialism. Born in 1875 to Hawaiian royalty (her mother was a princess) and a Scottish businessman, Ka'iulani grew up as the last heir apparent to the Hawaiian Kingdom, celebrated by her people as a symbol of hope for a proud nation. She was intelligent, cultured, and strikingly beautiful (Victorian newspapers couldn't get enough of her poise and style). If life were fair, she might have eventually become a beloved queen of a thriving island kingdom. Instead, fate dealt Ka'iulani a cruel hand: just as she was coming of age, the independence of her kingdom – and her own future – were snatched away in a whirlwind of imperial politics.

The trouble began when Ka'iulani was still a teenager studying abroad. In January 1893, while the princess was in Europe, a group of American sugar planters and businessmen (with an eye on Hawaii's profitable sugar and strategic location) decided to stage a coup. They, along with a contingent of U.S. Marines, overthrew Ka'iulani's aunt, Queen Lili'uokalani, and declared a provisional government. One day Hawaii was an independent monarchy; the next, it was effectively under the control of men like Sanford Dole (yes, of pineapple fame) who were lobbying to have Hawaii annexed to the United States. Imagine being 17 and reading in the papers that your home has been taken over and your throne (for which you've been groomed since birth) has vanished overnight. Ka'iulani hadn't even had her debutante ball yet, and suddenly her title meant nothing to the new regime. Talk about a rude awakening.

But our princess was no shrinking violet. With a courage that would put Disney heroines to shame, Ka'iulani sailed to the United States in 1893 to plead her nation's case. Dressed in Victorian elegance, she stood before American audiences and reporters and implored them to remember Hawaii's plight. The American press, rife with racist assumptions, had branded her a "dusky princess" and expected a naïve, unsophisticated girl – only to be stunned by her eloquence and grace in speaking multiple languages. She met President Grover Cleveland and made such an impression that he initially opposed annexation, calling the coup wrongful. For a brief moment, it looked like Ka'iulani might succeed in turning the tide with empathy and reason. Picture it: a teenage royal *owning* a room full of cynical politicians and journalists, basically saying "Hey, my people are not some barbarian tribe – we have a kingdom, and you're stealing it." It's the kind of scene that gives you goosebumps.

Unfortunately, politics is a tougher beast than public relations. The U.S. presidency soon passed to William McKinley, a man keen on expanding American territory. By 1898, amid the fervor of the Spanish–American War, the U.S. officially annexed Hawaii. Ka'iulani could only watch in heartbreak as Hawaii's flag was lowered for the last time and the Stars and Stripes raised. She and her aunt Lili'uokalani symbolically boycotted the annexation ceremony (choosing mourning dress over celebration), but the deed was done. Her kingdom was gone – absorbed into the United States, against the will of many Native Hawaiians.

Amid this national tragedy, Ka'iulani's personal life was also being steered by forces beyond her control. With the monarchy effectively dissolved, the question arose: what now for the princess? Her family and the remaining Hawaiian nobles still hoped to preserve some semblance of the royal lineage and dignity, so naturally they looked to that age-old strategy – marriage. In 1897, at age 21, Ka'iulani got engaged to Prince David Kawānanakoa, a high-ranking Hawaiian chief and her distant cousin. This engagement was more political than romantic; it was intended to unite two noble lines and bolster Hawaiian leadership in a time of uncertainty. Think of it as the last Hail Mary of a fading monarchy – if Hawaii couldn't have a queen, maybe at least the princess could marry a prince and keep hope alive. Ka'iulani, for her part, had always longed to marry for love. In fact, when pressed earlier about an arranged match, she once said, *"I feel it would be wrong if I married a man I did not love."* – a remarkably candid and modern sentiment for a royal woman of her time. But duty called, and ever the obedient daughter of her nation, she consented to the engagement.

It's worth noting that Ka'iulani's heart was heavy even as this plan unfolded. In private letters, she revealed that she had to break off a budding romance with an English suitor because of the expectation she'd marry strategically. "I must have been born under an unlucky star," she lamented, "as I seem to have my life planned out for me in such a way that I cannot alter it". That line reads like a poignant Victorian tweet (if they had Twitter in 1897) – #FateProblems, if you will. The "unlucky star" indeed: she was a princess who had every outward privilege, yet her freedom to choose her own happiness was smothered by both family obligation and international politics.

Sadly, the story grows only more tragic. Shortly after her engagement, Ka'iulani's health took a turn for the worse. She had endured years of stress – losing her mother young, the overthrow of her kingdom, exhausting diplomatic battles, and constant uncertainty. By 1898, friends noted she seemed fatigued and melancholic. That year, she caught a cold while out riding in the rain. In a normally healthy 23-year-old, it would have been a passing illness. But Ka'iulani had lost the will to live. The cold worsened to pneumonia, and her spirit, so drained by heartbreak and disappointment, could not fight it. She grew weaker through the winter of 1898–99. On March 6, 1899, Princess Ka'iulani died at just 23 years old, leaving her homeland and supporters in mourning. Her father, Archibald Cleghorn, in a moment of bitter resignation, said that it was *fitting* – since Hawai'i was lost, "Ka'iulani was lost as well." A poetic and painful epitaph if ever there was one.

Ka'iulani's short life was defined by loss on multiple levels. She lost her country, her throne, and her future role as queen. She lost the chance to marry the man she might have truly loved (whoever he was), and in the end, she lost her health and life, perhaps partly due to a broken heart. Yet, amid these losses, she showed incredible grace and grit. She fought with words and charm where others fought with guns, wielding empathy and intelligence in an attempt to protect her people. In our satirical recounting, we can't help but highlight the absurd contrasts: Here was a young woman who should have been planning balls and dress fittings, instead *lobbying the President of the United States* for her nation's sovereignty. It's as if a character from a Jane Austen novel wandered onto the set of *Game of Thrones*.

Humor in Ka'iulani's tale comes wrapped in irony. For example, one could quip that her life was like a Disney princess story written by a cynical historian. She had the animal companions (loads of peacocks at her Waikīkī estate), the sumptuous wardrobe, and admirers writing poems about her beauty – but the "happy ending" was snatched away by Uncle Sam wielding a treaty. It's a bit like *Moana* ending with the ocean being privatized by a U.S. shipping company – ridiculous and tragic at once. We can also marvel at the stiff Victorian logic she was up against: "Oh, the kingdom's fallen? Quick, marry the princess off to restore hope!" As if a wedding could stop an empire. The colonizers' audacity and the Hawaiian royals' desperation combined to script a fate that no rom-com writer would dare invent.

Through it all, a powerful lesson shines: empathy and emotional understanding were largely absent from the equation. The American businessmen didn't care about Hawaiian feelings or rights; to them, Hawaii was a prize, not a nation of real people. Even Ka'iulani's own elders, in pushing that dutiful engagement, gave precedence to political expediency over her personal feelings. Ka'iulani, for her part, tried to humanize the struggle – her speeches essentially said, "Put yourself in our shoes." She appealed to hearts, not just heads. And perhaps if more hearts had listened (in Washington, or in Honolulu), her life might have been longer and happier. Instead, her tragedy reminds us that when power ignores pain, even a princess can succumb to despair. In the end, Ka'iulani stands in history as a figure of *what could have been* – a bright light dimmed too soon, a princess who deserved a better destiny than the one she got. Her story, while satirically ripe with contrasts, leaves us with that sober truth: stealing someone's kingdom is bad, but stealing their hope is what truly breaks them.

Crown Prince Dipendra of Nepal – Love, Madness, and a Royal Massacre

Our final tale fast-forwards to the 21st century and ups the "tragic" factor to downright horrifying. If Rudolf and Ka'iulani's stories were operatic tragedies, the saga of Nepal's Crown Prince Dipendra is like a Shakespearean tragedy crossed with a true-crime thriller. It's proof that royal drama didn't vanish with the age of horse-drawn carriages – in fact, one of the most shocking royal scandals in history took place in 2001, within living memory, and it unfolded with the chaotic intensity of an action movie (one directed by Quentin Tarantino, perhaps).

Dipendra Bir Bikram Shah was the handsome, Oxford-educated crown prince of Nepal, beloved by the public and literally revered due to his divine royal status. (No, really – many Nepalis saw their king as an incarnation of the Hindu god Vishnu, so the crown prince was kind of a demigod in waiting. Talk about a god complex waiting to happen.) By all outward appearances, young Prince Dipendra was doing great. He was popular and even had a cute nickname, "Dippy," bestowed by the people. He trained at Eton in England – the same school that churns out British princes – and was known for being an excellent marksman and an academic achiever. If life were a fairy tale, Dipendra would have smoothly ascended the throne, married a princess, and lived regally ever after. Instead, his story took a dark, twisted turn that nobody saw coming (though hindsight, as always, reveals some warning signs).

The heart of the matter was Dipendra's love life. While in England, he fell in love with Devyani Rana, a beautiful young woman from a prominent Indian-Nepali aristocratic family. In another world, their union might have been seen as a strong alliance – Devyani was accomplished and from an influential clan. But in the archaic world of royal matchmaking, there was a catch: Devyani's family, the Ranas, though nobility, had some historical bad blood and different status from the Shah dynasty. Even more scandalizing for the Nepali royals, Devyani's grandfather had been an Indian *maharajah*. Cue the dramatic music – this was a problem for Queen Aishwarya (Dipendra's formidable mother), who sniffed at the match. The Queen had her own candidate for her son's bride: someone from within the extended royal family, a *"suitable"* princess who would maintain the pure bloodline. In other words, *"Sorry son, you can't marry the love of your life; she's not the right kind of royal."* Talk about a toxic mix of tradition and pride.

Dipendra, to put it mildly, was furious at his parents' rejection of Devyani. Here was a modern young man, educated abroad, probably thinking he could choose his own wife (like his commoner classmates could). Instead, he was being dragged into a medieval-style arranged marriage scenario against his will. The palace became a pressure cooker of arguments. By many accounts, it got so heated that the King and Queen threatened to disinherit Dipendra – basically cut him off from the throne – if he insisted on marrying Devyani. Imagine being told that your crown, your purpose since birth, will be taken away *and* you can't have the woman you love. That's a one-two emotional punch that would destabilize anyone. And Dipendra was not just anyone; he was a man who'd been treated as near-divine, probably not used to hearing "no."

On the night of June 1, 2001, this ticking time bomb of familial conflict detonated in the most appalling way. The extended royal family had gathered at the palace for a casual monthly dinner – uncles, aunts, cousins, all enjoying a relaxed evening in the Narayanhiti Royal Palace. Dipendra was present, and he was heavily intoxicated (reports say he'd had a lot to drink and possibly other substances). At some point during the evening, an argument erupted between Dipendra and his mother (presumably over, you guessed it, Devyani). His father, King Birendra – a gentle, well-respected king – grew angry and sent Dipendra to his room to cool off. This was no ordinary "You're grounded, young man," moment. The 29-year-old crown prince, humiliated and enraged, stumbled off... but he didn't stay put.

Instead, Dipendra returned armed to the teeth with multiple firearms. What followed is almost too horrific to be believed: Dipendra opened fire on his own family in a murderous rampage. In the span of a few minutes, he shot and killed nine people, including his father the King and his mother the Queen. Among the dead were also his younger brother and sister, plus several aunts, uncles, and other relatives. He nearly wiped out the entire royal line in one go – a real-life "Red Wedding" scenario that would later have the world's media aghast. As chaos reigned and blood stained the golden halls, Dipendra finally turned one of the guns on himself, attempting suicide.

Miraculously (and here's where reality is stranger than fiction), Dipendra did not die immediately. He was found comatose, with a self-inflicted gunshot wound, but still alive. With King Birendra dead, the Nepalese royal tradition dictated that Dipendra, as the crown prince, *became king* the moment his father expired. So, believe it or not, Nepal had a new king – King Dipendra – who was lying in a hospital bed on life support. For three surreal days, Nepal essentially had a comatose king. (If this were an episode of *The Crown*, nobody would buy the script!) As you can imagine, the nation was in a state of utter shock and confusion. People poured into the streets; some were furious, many were grief-stricken, most were in disbelief that the friendly prince they nicknamed "Dippy" could do something so heinous. Conspiracy theories blossomed: Was it really Dipendra who pulled the trigger, or was he being framed? Was it an accident? The palace initially even floated a story that the automatic weapon misfired *on its own*, which the public largely rejected as nonsense.

Dipendra died on June 4, 2001, never regaining consciousness. His uncle Gyanendra (the only senior royal absent at the dinner) then took the throne, making him the third king in three days for Nepal. But by then, the damage was irreversible – not just to the family, but to the very institution of monarchy. The Nepalese public, who once regarded their royals as near-deities, felt betrayed on an elemental level. How do you reconcile the idea of a King being a god when the Crown Prince just massacred his kin? The answer was: you don't. In the aftermath, the Nepalese monarchy's mystique was shattered. Riots broke out as citizens demanded answers. Over time, as the shock turned to disillusionment, a republican movement gained momentum. Within seven years, by 2008, Nepal abolished its monarchy and became a republic. It was the dramatic end of a 239-year-old royal dynasty – an end accelerated directly by Dipendra's night of carnage.

Now, it's challenging to find humor in an event so dark, but a satirical lens might focus on the ghastly *absurdity* of the circumstances. Consider the layers of irony: a prince, whose very upbringing was meant to exemplify control and honor, completely loses it over a love dispute. The institution designed to provide stability – the royal family – is wiped out by its own future head. And the *literal* gallows humor of Dipendra being king while in a coma cannot be overlooked. (One could imagine a macabre Monty Python sketch: "The King is dead, long live the King… who is unconscious and under armed guard in the ICU.") It's the ultimate tragic farce. If one of those old soothsayers had told the King "Your son will destroy your family and end the monarchy because you wouldn't let him marry his girlfriend," the King would've probably banished the fool for spouting nonsense. Yet here we are, with exactly that outcome.

The massacre also underscores, in the most violent way, the theme of mental health and unaddressed trauma. Clearly, Dipendra was a young man in immense turmoil. There were reports (later) that he had a "dual character" – outwardly pleasant, inwardly angry and disturbed. One palace official even reflected that Dipendra "probably didn't get the love he should have as a child." A simple statement, but an insightful one: Dipendra was raised with discipline and privilege, but perhaps not the kind of unconditional emotional support that might have helped him cope with personal setbacks. And in the insular royal bubble, where do you go with your grievances? It's not like the crown prince could book a therapist and talk about his feelings. The culture was one of stoicism, duty, and obedience, not open-hearted empathy. Queen Aishwarya's approach to her son's defiance was basically "Do as I say, or else," which poured gasoline on a fire. No one, it seems, truly tried to understand Dipendra's anguish—or if they did, they were overruled by those who thought upholding tradition was more important.

In terms of generational pressure, this tale is the ultimate cautionary example. King Birendra and Queen Aishwarya were by many accounts loving parents in a formal way, but when it came to the one choice Dipendra wanted to make for himself, they balked. They valued the *old ways* (marry your cousin, keep the bloodline pure) over their son's happiness. Dipendra, having tasted a bit of freedom abroad, just couldn't accept that. This was a collision course set by pride and a lack of communication. Had there been a willingness to compromise—or even to *truly listen*—maybe things would not have escalated. Instead, everyone dug in: the parents with their ultimatum, the son with his increasingly erratic, intoxicated brooding. It was a keg of gunpowder with no safety valve. In a grim twist of words, you could say Dipendra took "til death do us part" into his own hands, eliminating the family that opposed his love. That's not just tragic; it's a terrifying outburst of entitlement and pain.

For Nepal, the massacre became a national trauma that people are still processing decades later. Many Nepalis still speak of the event in hushed tones, and conspiracy theories linger because the truth—that a lovesick prince killed his family—is almost too painful to accept. But if we strip away the royal titles and mythology, we see an age-old story: a young man with unhealed emotional wounds, who felt cornered by family and fate, lashed out in the most destructive way possible. It's an extreme illustration of what can happen when empathy and understanding are absent. The royal palace in Kathmandu had walls adorned with portraits of gods and kings, but apparently no space for a heart-to-heart between a mother and son.

In a roundabout, horrific way, Dipendra's act did change his destiny and that of Nepal's. He didn't get to marry Devyani (who, for the record, went on to marry someone else and move on with life), but he sure ensured that *no one* in his family would tell him what to do ever again. It's dark, it's twisted, and it invites us to reflect on just how vital compassion is, especially among those with power. Because without it, even a palace can turn into a slaughterhouse.

Empathy – The Radical Cure That Never Was

Looking back on these three stories – Rudolf and Mary's Mayerling pact, Ka'iulani's broken heart and kingdom, Dipendra's night of madness – a common thread emerges through the satire and sorrow: a profound lack of empathy and emotional support in environments that desperately needed it. Each tale features people who, despite their lofty titles and opulent settings, were fundamentally *human* – vulnerable to despair, frustration, and anguish. And in each case, the people around them (be it family, advisors, or whole governments) failed to truly see and address that humanity.

Let's briefly unravel the thematic threads we've woven through these narratives:

- Loss: All our protagonists experienced devastating loss. Rudolf and Mary lost their lives (and the Habsburgs lost an heir) in a night of passion and despair. Ka'iulani lost her country, her crown, and eventually her life – a cascade of losses that began with imperial greed. Dipendra, in a twisted inversion, caused an immense loss – he destroyed his own family and, indirectly, the centuries-old monarchy. In every case, the losses weren't just personal; they echoed in national histories and collective memories.

- Mental Health: None of these tragedies can be separated from the psychological states of the people involved. Rudolf was reportedly depressed and spiraling, essentially a royal stuck in a gilded cage of expectations. Ka'iulani suffered what we'd now recognize as clinical depression (losing the will to live is a big red flag in any era) amid immense stress. Dipendra's homicidal breakdown was the violent climax of long-simmering mental and emotional turmoil – a prince under unbearable pressure who chose a path of destruction. In their times, "mental health" wasn't part of the vocabulary; there were no counsellors in the palace, no safe spaces to talk about feelings. The prevailing attitude was *"Keep calm and carry on (and for heaven's sake, don't scandalize the court)"*. The tragic outcomes illustrate how ignoring mental health can literally be deadly.

- Colonialism & External Pressures: The force of impersonal history bulldozed the individuals in these stories. Ka'iulani's fate was sealed not by personal failure but by the machinery of colonialism, which cared nothing for her dreams. Rudolf lived in an empire on the brink – the Austro-Hungarian Empire was creaking under ethnic tensions and old-school rigidity, and those macro pressures surely weighed on a reform-minded prince. (In some ways, Rudolf's liberal ideas were crushed by the reactionary climate around him, just as his love was crushed by protocol.) For Dipendra, the "external" pressure was tradition and the expectation of the monarchy – Nepal wasn't colonized by a foreign power, but one could say he was colonized by *custom*, invaded by the rigid demands of his royal heritage. Each story shows an individual caught in the gears of something bigger – be it empire, monarchy, or archaic customs.

- Generational Conflict: Ah, the classic parent-child drama, but amplified by crowns and treaties. We see fathers and mothers versus sons and daughters. Franz Joseph vs. Rudolf: the strict emperor who couldn't bend, and the son who couldn't stand straight under that weight. Lili'uokalani (and the Hawaiian chiefs) vs. Ka'iulani: elders trying to use a young woman as a pawn to fix what *they* had lost – well-meaning perhaps, but ultimately blind to her personal needs. King Birendra & Queen Aishwarya vs. Dipendra: parents whose refusal to adapt to their son's wishes led to everyone's undoing. These were not ordinary family squabbles over curfew or career choices; they were clashes over duty vs. happiness, tradition vs. personal truth. In each case, the older generation imposed its will, and the younger generation suffered mightily – a reminder that authoritarian family dynamics can be as deadly as any political rivalry.

So, where does that leave us? Are these just sad stories to sigh over? In a way, yes – but they're also cautionary tales that underscore a timeless moral: *Empathy* might have changed everything. Imagine, for a moment, an alternate timeline:

- Emperor Franz Joseph sits down with Rudolf and says, "My son, tell me what's in your heart," instead of essentially ordering him to dump Mary Vetsera. Maybe Rudolf would have felt heard, maybe Mary's life would have been spared, and maybe the Habsburgs would have avoided the black stain of Mayerling.

- The American powers listen to Princess Ka'iulani's plea and say, "You know what, annexation can wait – these people deserve their freedom." Hawaii's story would be vastly different, and a young princess might not have withered from grief. Or even on the personal level, what if Ka'iulani's inner circle had said, "You've sacrificed so much; marry whom you want, do what makes *you* happy"? It sounds almost fanciful given the era, but one empathetic choice might have given her a chance at real joy.

- King Birendra and Queen Aishwarya could have told Dipendra, "We don't like your choice, but we love you, so let's figure this out." Perhaps a compromise could be found, or at least the prince wouldn't have felt like an enemy in his own house. A tough conversation, some understanding, and who knows – the worst night in Nepal's history might have been averted.

These hypotheticals boil down to people in power showing a little heart. That's why we say empathy would have been *radical* in these contexts – it went against the grain of stiff royal protocol and imperial arrogance. But radical or not, it was the missing ingredient that could have saved lives and heartache.

In retelling these stories with a bit of wit and irreverence, we're not laughing at the misfortunes – we're highlighting the human absurdity in them to drive home this point. It *is* absurd that an empire's heir felt so isolated he chose death over life. It's absurd that a princess fluent in four languages and loved by all had to *beg* for her nation's dignity and died despondent. It's absurd that a crown prince with the world at his feet would murder the very family that raised him. Absurd – and yet, when we look around at our world, not inexplicable. Lack of empathy, unchecked ego, zero mental health support – that trifecta can and does lead to tragedy in any era.

In closing, if there's a silver lining to derive, it's a renewed appreciation for kindness and understanding. History, with all its pageantry, often forgets to mention the gentle voices that might have spoken but didn't. Let's not forget: behind every crown is a person who laughs, loves, and can break down just like the rest of us. Destiny denied these royals their happiness, but perhaps *we* can learn from their fates. The next time someone's hurting or boxed in by life, a little empathy from us might be the lifeline that changes their story. After all, if empathy can prevent even one tragic ending, then it truly is a powerful, radical force – mightier than any empire, and more transformative than any crown.

And if nothing else, at least we've seen that history isn't all stodgy dates and treaties; it's full of real people with real emotions. Sometimes they're funny, sometimes they're heartbreaking. In our three stories, they were both, and through that mix of humor and heartache, we find a compassionate truth: *no one*, not even princes and princesses, should have to face their demons alone. Let's remember that chuckle at the ironies, and hope we can do better with our own destinies.

Chapter 6

The Art of Divorce –
Royals Who Broke the Mold

W hen you think of royal marriages, you might picture fairytale
weddings, glittering tiaras, and "happily ever after" engraved
in stone. But what happens when the ever after isn't so happy?
Historically, kings and queens stayed hitched come hell or high water
(or *Anne Boleyn lost her head* – literally, in Henry VIII's case).
Divorce was once the ultimate royal taboo; monarchs would rather
start new religions or renounce thrones than sign divorce papers.
Fast-forward to the late 20th century, and a few bold royals decided
to do the unthinkable: call it quits. In this chapter, we explore three
cases of "I do" turning into "I don't anymore" – with a cheeky twist.
From the British icon who turned a doomed marriage into a global
cause célèbre, to a Jordanian queen who modernized a kingdom (and
had *James Bond* rumors swirling), to progressive Swedish royals
quietly normalizing divorce like it's no big deal, these stories show
that ending a royal union can be an act of courage and
transformation, not just a scandal. So, grab your popcorn (or a cuppa
tea) as we dive into *The Art of Divorce – Royals Who Broke the Mold*.

Princess Diana and Prince Charles – A Fairytale Crash and Modern Revival

Once upon a time in 1981, Lady Diana Spencer married Prince Charles in a ceremony so lavish it made Cinderella's ball look like open-mic night. The world swooned over Diana's poufy taffeta gown and the golden carriage ride through London. She was 20, shy, and deemed the *"perfect"* royal bride – basically the Taylor Swift of aristocracy, with endless chart-topping charm. Prince Charles, heir to the British throne, was her slightly awkward Prince Charming. But this story didn't stick to the script of *happily ever after*. Instead, it turned into a royal soap opera with more twists than an entire season of *The Crown*. By the end, our fairytale princess had rewritten the narrative of what it means to exit a royal marriage with grace, guts, and a dash of irreverence.

From the get-go, cracks showed in the picture-perfect image. The couple's 13-year age gap was palpable; Diana was an innocent kindergarten teacher, while Charles was a world-traveled prince pushing mid-thirties, already set in his ways (and still chatting with his plants). Then there was the not-so-small matter of Camilla Parker Bowles, Charles's longtime love, lurking in the background like the proverbial elephant in the palace. Diana later famously quipped, *"Well, there were three of us in this marriage, so it was a bit crowded."* That single sentence – delivered with a mix of poise and sass in her 1995 BBC Panorama interview – ricocheted around the world and landed like a bombshell in the House of Windsor. It's the kind of line that would make a killer movie tagline (and indeed it has, in countless documentaries). For the first time, a royal wife publicly called out her husband's infidelity and the *"other woman"*, shattering the illusion that royal marriages were storybook-perfect. The monarchy's stiff upper lip positively trembled.

If the palace hoped Diana would suffer in silence as unhappy royal wives of yore did, they had vastly underestimated her. This was the 1980s and 90s – the era of Margaret Thatcher, Madonna, and a rising tide of female agency – and Diana was not about to remain a voiceless figurehead. At first, she tried to conform to the ideal: the demure princess, raising two adored princes (William and Harry), smiling dutifully for the cameras. But behind palace doors, she battled postnatal depression and bulimia, and felt desperately lonely in her gilded cage. The media, however, sensed *drama* and pounced like paparazzi (literally). The British tabloids began dubbing the marital rift "The War of the Waleses", turning the implosion of Charles and Di's relationship into front-page spectator sport. Imagine the pressures of any young couple's marriage – then add headlines, photographers hiding in bushes, and the knowledge that 750 million people watched your wedding so they're *definitely* invested in your marriage. It was a royal pressure cooker set to explode.

Princess Diana dancing with John Travolta at the White House, 1985. This iconic image captured Diana's star power and individuality apart from her royal marriage, as she twirled across the floor with a Hollywood actor at a Reagan-era gala. The scene – orchestrated by Nancy Reagan for maximum glam – showed a confident princess charming the world on her own terms. Diana's ability to connect, whether with movie stars or ordinary people, made her a media superstar and foreshadowed her break from traditional royal restraints. In moments like this, it was clear that Diana was not just a supporting player in a royal fairy tale; she was the leading lady of her own story, captivating a global audience.

By the early 1990s, the facade of a united royal couple had completely shattered. In 1992 – dubbed "Annus Horribilis" by the Queen for good reason – Charles and Diana formally separated. Tabloid leaks poured out: Diana's intimate phone chats, Charles's private musings, *Camillagate* tapes (cringe-worthy transcripts of Charles cooing endearments to Camilla – we'll spare you the details). It was messy, undignified, and utterly riveting to the public. For a monarchy that had survived beheadings, revolutions, and abdications, a little divorce shouldn't have been a biggie – but in modern times, this was unprecedented. No heir to the British throne had gotten divorced in modern history. The last time a monarch-in-waiting tried to marry a divorcee (King Edward VIII in 1936), he had to abdicate the crown and *flee* to France. Yet here was the Queen's own son heading for Splitsville, and the monarchy couldn't pretend everything was fine. Talk about modernization via personal crisis.

What's remarkable (and inspiring) is how Diana took control of her narrative during this turbulence. Instead of fading into obedient obscurity, she transformed into a *people's champion*. In that explosive 1995 TV interview, she spoke candidly about her pain, her *"crowded"* marriage, and even her own infidelity, showing a human vulnerability that royals typically kept under lock and key. This wasn't just airing dirty laundry; it was Diana reclaiming her voice. By 1996, the divorce was official – Queen Elizabeth II reportedly gave the green light after the Panorama interview made reconciliation impossible. Diana relinquished the title "Her Royal Highness" but kept the more meaningful one: "Princess of Wales." And in public opinion, she only grew more beloved. Freed from the stifling constraints of palace life, Diana seemed to come into her own. She dedicated herself to charitable causes with a zeal that embarrassed the stuffier royals. Abolishing landmines? Visiting AIDS patients and shaking hands without gloves? Comforting leprosy victims? Unheard of for a princess before her – but Diana did it all, and in high heels. *The very traits that had made her "difficult" as a wife – her emotional openness, empathy, and independent streak – became her greatest strengths as an individual.* She truly became, as she hoped, the Queen of People's Hearts (with apologies to Her Majesty).

In the process, Diana dragged the monarchy kicking and screaming into the 20th century (just in time for the 21st). *"In life and death, Princess Diana modernised the monarchy,"* as one analysis put it, shaking the House of Windsor to its foundations in a media-driven age. She gave the royal family a much-needed reality check. The monarchy had long been perceived as aloof and inflexible, but Diana's influence forced a rethink. Jenni Bond, a former BBC royal correspondent, noted that Diana *"gave the monarchy a jolt…determined to make it less remote"*. Indeed, many of the more human, approachable gestures we see from royals now – hugging children on walkabouts, speaking openly about mental health, etc. – trace back to Diana's legacy. *"She was behind a lot of modernisation,"* said biographer Penny Junor; the way the royals do things today is largely influenced by Diana's impact. In other words, by breaking the mold – and eventually breaking free of her unhappy marriage – Diana reinvented what it meant to be a royal in the modern world.

Of course, her story ended in tragedy: Diana's death in 1997, fleeing paparazzi in Paris, was the final gut-punch in this saga. But even in death, she spurred change. The public outpouring of grief (and outrage at the royal family's initial stiff response) compelled the Queen to publicly address the nation – an unprecedented move – and acknowledge Diana's special place in people's hearts. The monarchy learned, belatedly, that it *must* bend with the times or risk breaking entirely. Diana's sons, William and Harry, have carried forward many of her values, from charitable initiatives to a more down-to-earth approach with the public. One could argue that even Harry and Meghan's 2020 royal exit (often cheekily dubbed *"Megxit"*) drew on the trail Diana blazed: prioritizing personal well-being over institutional duty, and not tolerating a toxic media environment. Diana showed that a royal divorce, once unthinkable, could be a story of personal empowerment rather than just failure. She took a wrecked fairy tale and built a real life – one with purpose, passion, and yes, flaws, but *her own*. In doing so, she changed the monarchy more than any dutiful princess ever could.

Queen Noor and King Hussein – An American Queen in a Modernizing Kingdom

When Lisa Najeeb Halaby – a Princeton-educated, all-American woman – married King Hussein of Jordan in 1978, it sounded like a script Disney might have rejected for being *too* far-fetched. A 26-year-old Arab-American socialite meets a Middle Eastern monarch, and he whisks her into a new life as Queen Noor al-Hussein ("Light of Hussein")? It's the kind of modern fairy tale that could only happen in real life. If Princess Diana's saga was a rock-and-roll soap opera, Queen Noor's story was more of a cultural dramedy – *"An American in Amman"* – complete with grand romance, cultural collisions, palace intrigues, and a heroine determined to find her voice. While

Noor's marriage to King Hussein did not end in divorce (she was his fourth and final wife, and they stayed together until his death), she *did* break the mold of what a queen consort could be. Her challenges were less about marital strife and more about modernizing expectations and asserting female agency in a traditional royal framework. In a sense, Queen Noor divorced the stereotypical role of a silent, ornamental queen and transformed it into something far more impactful.

The backstory reads like a Hollywood meet-cute: Lisa Halaby, born in Washington, D.C., was the daughter of a prominent Arab-American family (her dad was CEO of Pan Am and a former head of the FAA). She was brainy and ambitious – a Princeton architecture graduate – and moved to the Middle East to work on urban planning projects in the 1970s. Picture this young American woman in flared jeans and hard hat, giving design advice on a Jordanian palace. That's literally how she met King Hussein: she was consulting on his palace's landscaping when the charismatic, twice-divorced king noticed her. Sparks flew across the *schematic diagrams*, so to speak. Hussein proposed, Lisa converted to Islam, and suddenly this California-born, chocolate-chip-cookie-baking gal was Her Majesty Queen Noor of Jordan. If you think *The Princess Diaries* had a steep learning curve, imagine trading a free-spirited American life for a throne in a conservative monarchy overnight.

Noor happily embraced the role of Hussein's partner on the world stage – she wasn't dragged unwillingly to the altar. But she soon learned that being a modern, outspoken queen could ruffle some feathers. On day one, she became a media sensation just by virtue of who she was. The Jordanian public and the international press were intensely curious about this chic blond American who suddenly appeared in King Hussein's life. Noor was excited to use her platform for meaningful causes, but early on, the media seemed more interested in her fashion and background than her ideas. On her first official visit to Washington as queen, reporters lobbed softball questions about her clothes and lifestyle, ignoring the substantive issues she cared about. Noor was *miffed*. *"I hoped to be taken as a credible voice with serious matters to discuss,"* she later wrote, expressing her frustration that the press focused on trivia instead of, say, her views on development or peace. It was a classic monarchy-vs-media clash, updated for the modern age: the queen wanted to talk about women's education and refugee aid, while the media wanted to know where she bought her shoes.

To be fair, Noor's arrival did come with plenty of tabloid-ready drama. As a foreigner and a commoner (and American to boot), she had to win over a skeptical Jordanian public and royal family. Early on, some Jordanians bristled at her perceived lavish tastes. Gossip circulated about her love of shopping and designer clothes – portraying her as *more Beverly Hills than Bedouin*. (One nasty rumor claimed she had a nose job and hid from cameras for weeks; the state-controlled press was even allegedly told not to publish her photos during recovery – a very L.A. move for a queen!) The most scandalous chatter involved Sir Sean Connery – yes, James Bond himself. When Connery visited Jordan in the late '80s to film *Indiana Jones and the Last Crusade*, Noor struck up a friendly rapport with the silver-haired star. *Cue the rumor mill:* suddenly everyone was *"openly gossiping about the close friendship"* the queen had with Connery on set. It got so absurd that a Jordanian embassy spokesman had to publicly call the rumors *"ridiculous,"* dismissing any suggestion of impropriety. Imagine, the dignified Queen Noor being shipped in tabloids with 007 – it was the kind of surreal pop-culture crossover the media *loved*, and the palace *hated*.

Behind the lurid headlines, Noor was navigating more profound challenges. She was a queen consort in a region where that role typically involved looking elegant, producing heirs, and not stirring the pot. But Noor was, by nature, a pot-stirrer – in the best way. She threw herself into charitable and humanitarian work, focusing on education, women's empowerment, and culture. Early in her queenship, she established the Noor Al-Hussein Foundation, aiming to uplift Jordan's most vulnerable citizens (with a particular focus on women and children). She championed women-in-development programs to help integrate women into Jordan's economy, and she talked openly about environmental issues and refugees – not exactly light, apolitical topics. Over two decades, Noor helped implement ambitious plans to improve Jordanians' quality of life. Her official website could practically be a novella, listing *reams of charitable initiatives* from landmine removal to arts education. In a way, she was performing a delicate balancing act: bringing Western-style activism and candor into an Eastern royal court, all while remaining respectful of cultural norms. It didn't always go smoothly, but she made tangible progress and earned respect over time.

Noor's female agency was evident in how she defined her identity beyond just "the King's wife." She juggled being a queen, a mother of four, and an international public figure with aplomb (and occasional awkwardness, as she admits). After King Hussein's death in 1999, Noor found herself in a unique position: a dowager queen with no throne, straddling two worlds. She moved back to the U.S. part-time, raised her kids, and continued global advocacy – essentially crafting a second act for herself. A Washington Post profile in 2004 described her living in suburban Virginia, sipping ginger tea in jeans and a sweater, leading a relatively normal life one moment and then jetting off to dine with Nelson Mandela or consult with Kofi Annan the next. *"Nothing here screams 'royalty' – no tiaras, no bowing servants,"* the reporter noted of her stateside home, highlighting how Noor managed to be both regal and down-to-earth. She was candid about trying to *"live a normal life"* while still using her experience for public service. *"I'm always going to be instinctively a private person and also motivated to be a public servant,"* Noor reflected, acknowledging the paradox of her post-queen existence. It's a line that could apply to *any* modern royal woman redefining her role (hello, Meghan Markle), and Noor was doing it before it was cool.

Looking at Noor's journey, it's clear that modernization and female empowerment were at the heart of her story. She didn't divorce King Hussein, but in many ways she divorced the *traditional expectations* of a Middle Eastern royal consort. She carved out an influence based on intellect and compassion, not just pedigree. There were hiccups and scandals, sure – the *Mean Girls* of the Amman gossip circuit had their field days – but Noor endured and evolved. She even wrote a bestselling memoir telling her side of the story (aptly titled "Leap of Faith" – because leaping into Hussein's world certainly required one). Through it all, she maintained a sharp wit and resilience. In public, she was poised and elegant; in private, friends say she could be irreverent and humorous about the absurdities of royal life. One could easily imagine Queen Noor joking, *"I have one foot in*

D.C. and one in Amman – it's a heck of a split, but at least I get to wear jeans in one of those places."

Ultimately, Noor's tale reinforces the chapter's moral: ending or changing a royal marriage (or role) can be about courage and transformation. Noor transformed the concept of a queen in Jordan. By being outspoken, hands-on, and globally engaged, she showed that a royal woman could be both a devoted wife *and* an independent force for good. She faced down media scrutiny and societal expectations, emerging as a respected humanitarian. In doing so, she helped drag a traditional monarchy a little further into modernity – not by burning bridges, but by building new ones (often literally, through her development projects). If Diana modernized the British monarchy through dramatic rebellion, Noor did it through gradual evolution and bridge-building. Both approaches took guts. Both women, each in their own way, proved that a tiara can sit on the head of a *real* person with passions and principles – and that sometimes the bravest thing a royal can do is break the mold.

Swedish Royals and 20th-Century Divorces – Scandals in Scandinavia, Done Sensibly

Compared to the high-octane drama of British and Jordanian courts, the Swedish royal family might *seem* downright placid. No worldwide media frenzy, no Hollywood stars in the mix – just Volvo-driving, IKEA-furniture-buying monarchs with sensible smiles. But don't be fooled by Scandinavian calm. In the 20th century, the Swedes were quietly pulling off progressive moves that put them ahead of the curve on royal relationship shake-ups. This is, after all, the nation that gave us ABBA – and as any fan knows, ABBA's lyrics have a breakup song for every occasion. (In fact, *"Knowing Me, Knowing You"* could be the soundtrack to some of these royal splits: *"Breaking up is never easy, I know…"*). The Swedish royals handled divorce with a kind of pragmatic, no-fuss attitude that is *so* very Nordic. In doing so, they modernized their monarchy without the global fanfare, and allowed their princes and princesses to put personal happiness above archaic rules. Let's dig into a couple of their most intriguing marital shake-ups, full of courage, a bit of scandal, and a surprising amount of Swedish sensibility.

Our first tale features a Russian Grand Duchess whose royal marriage in Sweden went up in smoke long before it was fashionable. Grand Duchess Maria Pavlovna "the Younger" of Russia was a bona fide member of the Romanov dynasty – cousin to Tsar Nicholas II – who married Sweden's Prince Wilhelm in 1908. It was a classic dynastic union: East meets North in a grand palatial wedding. Maria, just 18 at the time, found herself whisked from the splendor of Saint Petersburg to the much smaller (and, in her opinion, *duller*) Swedish court. To put it mildly, she did not *vibe* with Swedish royal life. She felt she had married beneath her imperial status (Wilhelm was a younger son of the king, and not *quite* up to her lofty standards). She even insisted that palace servants address her as "Your Imperial and Royal Highness" – outranking her husband's mere "Royal Highness," an egotistical flex that caused much eye-rolling in Stockholm. King Gustav V, Wilhelm's father, begrudgingly agreed that, yes, in terms of protocol Maria technically outranked his son (talk about awkward father-in-law duty). So, from day one, this was not your average harmonious royal couple; it was more like an aristocratic odd couple sitcom.

Things went from bad to worse. The marriage produced one son, Lennart, but no happiness. Maria found the Swedish court stifling and even traumatizing. The final straw was truly scandalous for its era: Maria alleged that the Swedish royal family's trusted physician, Dr. Axel Munthe, *had sexually accosted her,* and that the family basically shrugged it off and continued supporting the doctor. (*Yes, you read that right. MeToo, 1910s edition.*) Maria was *horrified* – she later described "the horror she felt toward the Swedish royal family" for siding with Munthe. In an era when royals were expected to grin-and-bear-it no matter what, Maria said "nej tack" (no thanks) and bolted. She sought a divorce, causing a sensation across Europe. Relatives on both sides realized the marriage was beyond saving, and by March 1914 the divorce was officially granted – with the sign-off of Sweden's King and Maria's cousin Tsar Nicholas II himself, who issued an edict approving the split. It was one of the first high-profile royal divorces in European 20th-century history. And guess what? The sky did *not* fall. Sweden did not collapse into anarchy. In fact, Swedes largely greeted the news with a collective shrug (and perhaps a polite toast of aquavit in private sympathy). There was no national crisis – just a tacit understanding that an unhappy princess had the right to chart her own destiny.

Grand Duchess Maria Pavlovna (Princess Wilhelm of Sweden) in 1912. In this photograph, the young Russian-born princess exudes confidence and a hint of defiance beneath her elaborate hat. Maria's aristocratic poise belied the turmoil in her marriage. By 1914, she shocked the royal world by divorcing Prince Wilhelm – an act almost unheard of for a princess of her era. The Swedish court may have found her hard to handle (she was, after all, unapologetically *Imperial* in attitude), but Maria's bold exit was a statement of agency. Rather than remain trapped in a miserable union, she chose freedom, escaping the "dull" Swedish court for a new life. Her story became legendary, illustrating that even a century ago a royal woman could break away and reinvent herself.

Maria Pavlovna's post-divorce life was itself a dramatic adventure. She returned to Russia just in time for World War I, served as a Red Cross nurse, and witnessed the Bolshevik Revolution that toppled her Romanov relatives. (Talk about trading one tumult for another!) She managed to flee revolutionary Russia with her jewelry sewn into her clothes – a princess-turned-refugee scenario straight out of an epic novel. Eventually she settled in Paris, started a chic embroidery business, and even wrote memoirs detailing her extraordinary life. In her books *"The Education of a Princess"* and *"A Princess in Exile"*, she didn't hold back about her failed Swedish marriage and the reasons she *had* to get out. Decades later, people came to view Maria not as a scandalous deserter of duty, but as a woman of remarkable courage who lived on her own terms. She even found love again (albeit briefly – her second marriage also ended in divorce, because apparently one divorce wasn't trailblazing enough for her!). And fun fact: her son Lennart, whom she left in Sweden to be raised by his father, grew up to be a bit of a rebel himself. Lennart fell in love with a commoner in the 1930s and, when told he couldn't marry her and keep his royal title, he said "Fine, keep your title" and married her anyway – promptly getting *stripped* of his prince status. The apple didn't fall far from the tree in terms of independent streaks.

In fact, the Swedish royal family saw multiple such cases of royals putting personal happiness first, even if it meant giving up status.

They were quietly progressive that way. Consider Prince Sigvard Bernadotte, King Gustav V's grandson. In 1934, Sigvard fell head over heels for a non-royal woman, a German commoner named Erika. This was a big no-no under the old royal house rules. But Sigvard, an artistically inclined sort (more interested in design than duty), went ahead and married Erika anyway. As expected, the punishment came: Prince Sigvard was stripped of his princely title and became plain Mr. Bernadotte, just like that. It sounds dramatic, but Sigvard didn't flinch. He essentially divorced his royal title in exchange for love, a move almost unthinkable at the time – and yet notably similar to what his cousin, Britain's King Edward VIII, would do two years later (Edward abdicated in 1936 to marry Wallis Simpson, a divorced American). In other words, a Swedish royal beat a British royal to the punch on sacrificing crown for romance. Sigvard went on to have a prolific career as a designer (one of his passions – he helped bring Scandinavian modern design to the world) and lived to a ripe old 94, happily married to his third wife. Sweden eventually softened too – in 1983, the King restored Sigvard's ducal title (though not the prince title) as a sort of olive branch. By then, the idea that a royal might marry a commoner without causing an empire to fall had become far more accepted, thanks to trailblazers like Sigvard.

There's also the example of Princess Birgitta (sister of the current King Carl XVI Gustaf) who in the 1960s married a German prince. Their marriage later fell apart and they separated (though never formally divorced), and Birgitta spent much of her life doing her own thing, golfing under the Spanish sun rather than performing royal duties in Stockholm. And King Carl Gustaf's other sister, Princess Margaretha, married a British businessman in the '60s and, after decades of marriage, they quietly separated in the '90s (remaining married on paper until his death, but essentially living apart). What's telling is how unfussy these situations were. No constitutional crises, no exile to distant continents. The Swedish public and press didn't turn these personal issues into a circus. Perhaps it's the cultural penchant for lagom – the concept of balance and moderation. The Swedes seemed to take the attitude: "Alright, that didn't work out, life goes on." In a parliamentary democracy where the monarchy had long ago been stripped of real power, a royal divorce wasn't seen as the end of the world. If anything, it made the royals seem more human and relatable. By the late 20th century, the Swedish royal house had even updated its laws to be more modern – for example, adopting absolute primogeniture in 1980 so that King Carl Gustaf's eldest child (Crown Princess Victoria) could inherit the throne regardless of gender. That move toward gender equality in succession was in the same spirit as accepting that marriages sometimes end: it was realism and modernization trumping old-fashioned convention.

Let's not pretend there was zero gossip – of course people whispered about Maria's dramatic exit or Sigvard's morganatic marriage. There were probably snarky cartoons in Swedish papers and disapproving tut-tuts at royal dinner tables. But notably, Sweden's monarchy endured these divorces and marriages to commoners without a dent in its stability. In fact, some would argue it made the monarchy *more* resilient by making it more in tune with ordinary citizens' lives. After all, by the late 20th century, divorce was hardly unusual in society at large. Why should royals be trapped in unhappy marriages when their subjects weren't? By having a few royals break the ice, the Bernadotte family showed it could adapt to the times – in a typically understated Scandinavian way, of course.

One deliciously ironic anecdote: in 1976, when Sweden's current King married Silvia Sommerlath (a commoner and former Olympic hostess from Germany), guess what music played at their gala? ABBA, performing "Dancing Queen" live for the royal couple. A commoner becoming Queen set to a pop song – talk about a sign of changing times. Today, all of King Carl XVI Gustaf's children have married commoners (with zero controversy), and divorce doesn't carry the stigma it once did. Princess Madeleine (the King's younger daughter) even broke off an engagement very publicly in 2010 and later married a British-American financier – all handled with relative calm. It's as if the Swedish monarchy long ago decided to quietly let go of the fairytale script and embrace something more authentic and sustainable.

In sum, the Swedish royals' approach to marital breakups was less flashy than the Brits', but arguably more forward-thinking. They treated these divorces not as failures of duty, but as personal matters – and allowed those involved (especially the women like Maria Pavlovna) to transform their lives thereafter. Maria Pavlovna, by leaving an untenable marriage, went on to find her purpose in a way she never could have as an unhappy Swedish princess. Sigvard and Lennart, by stepping outside royal rules, pursued fulfilling creative lives. The House of Bernadotte showed that a monarchy could bend without breaking, adjusting its expectations to align with modern values of individual happiness.

Throughout these stories – Diana's high-profile breakup that humanized a dynasty, Noor's cultural balancing act and redefinition of queenly duty, and the Swedish royals' quietly revolutionary divorces – a common thread emerges. Ending a royal marriage can be an act of courage and self-transformation. It's not a failure so much as a bold renegotiation of one's destiny. These royals broke the mold by saying *enough* to situations that were suffocating or unjust, even under the glare of public scrutiny and centuries of tradition pressuring them to keep calm and carry on (unhappily). And in doing so, they each sparked change. They showed that monarchies, those age-old institutions often perceived as rigid, can evolve – one personal decision at a time.

The media, of course, played its dual role: tormentor on the one hand, amplifier of their voices on the other. Diana was hounded by cameras, yet she shrewdly used her media platform to expose truths and elicit empathy. Noor bristled at shallow press coverage, yet ultimately cultivated a public image as a serious global advocate that even gossip couldn't diminish. The Swedish royals didn't have the same tabloid microscopes, but their willingness to quietly defy norms surely influenced other royals across Europe (and gave the press less to feast on by treating it matter-of-factly). In the tug-of-war between Monarchy vs. Media, these royals sometimes got burned, but also learned to bend the narrative in their favor – turning from victims of scandal into symbols of resilience.

At the heart of it all are themes of modernization and female agency. It's no coincidence that the most compelling figures in these tales are the women – Diana, Noor, Maria – who seized their agency in environments that often sought to suppress it. They each, in their own style, said: *I am more than a wife, more than a decorative royal appendage.* Diana found an identity as a humanitarian superstar once freed from an incompatible marriage. Noor proved she could be both a modern career woman and a traditional queen – but on her own terms, not as a silent partner. Maria Pavlovna, a century ago, walked away from royal status to preserve her dignity and sanity, blazing a trail for women's right to choose personal freedom over protocol. These acts were revolutionary in context. They nudged their royal houses – and societies – toward a more enlightened view that women (even royal women) are not pawns or prisoners of marriage. Female agency gained a foothold behind palace walls thanks to their examples.

Finally, through a moral lens, we see that a royal divorce or separation need not be seen as a *dishonoring* of fairy tale ideals, but rather as a courageous step toward authenticity and personal growth. There's a saying that goes, *"Sometimes the most revolutionary thing you can do is simply tell the truth about your life."* Diana told the truth about her marriage and forever changed how the public relates to the royals – injecting honesty and emotional intelligence where once stood façades. Noor told the truth that she was both East and West, both private person and public servant, and carved a new space for herself that transcended traditional labels. The Swedes quietly acknowledged the truth that love and compatibility matter more than tiaras and titles, and adjusted the monarchy to fit real human lives rather than forcing humans to fit the monarchy's dated molds.

So, what's the takeaway? In the grand tapestry of royal history, divorces and breakups were once ugly little knots to be hidden. But these stories reframe them as pivot points – moments when royals proved they have hearts that seek fulfillment just like anyone else. Ending a marriage, especially under public gaze, is never easy. Yet, by doing so with courage, a sense of purpose, and even a dash of humor, these royals turned personal trials into transformative journeys. They proved that even in the rarefied world of crowns and protocols, it's possible to find *freedom in truth*. And sometimes, stepping out of a royal marriage isn't the end of the fairy tale at all – it's the beginning of a new, more honest story. Knowing me, knowing you, as ABBA would say, "it's the best I can do."

Chapter 7

Love in Exile –
Banished, But Not Broken

Introduction: Royals Without a Realm

Once upon a time, in lands of gilded thrones and lofty titles, a few royals discovered that life is *really* interesting when the crown slips off. We often imagine kings and queens at balls and banquets, not scraping by in foreign cottages or plotting comebacks over tea. Yet history serves up some wild tales of monarchs who got a one-way ticket out of their kingdoms – and found out what they and their loved ones were truly made of.

In this chapter, we're going to time-travel through three such stories: the exiled *impératrice* Eugénie and her Emperor hubby Napoleon III making a new home in England; King Simeon II of Bulgaria going from child monarch to elder statesman (with a few decades of *"ex-king seeks day job"* in between); and King Constantine II of Greece with Queen Anne-Marie, an adventurous couple who learned that marriage vows sometimes include *"in exile and in health."* Each story flows into the next, tied together by a common theme: loyalty, resilience, and love outside the palace walls.

But don't expect a dry lecture – we're spicing this up with humor, modern analogies, and a healthy dose of royal sass. Think of it as *The Crown* meets *Survivor* meets a history roast. After all, true character isn't revealed when you're on a throne; it's revealed when you're *thrown* – into exile, that is. So, grab your popcorn (or a cup of extremely strong coffee, if you're Empress Eugénie) and enjoy these intertwined tales of love in exile.

The Imperial Exit: Eugénie and Napoleon III's Second Act

Empress Eugénie and her son, the Prince Imperial, find a moment of calm in an English garden during their exile in the 1870s.

September 1870, Paris – Empress Eugénie is having a *really* bad day. Picture this: one moment you're hosting lavish soirées at the Tuileries; the next, you're fleeing an angry mob with nothing but the gown on your back and maybe a few crown jewels stuffed in your purse. How did it come to this? Well, her husband Napoleon III had decided to declare war on Prussia in a fit of imperial overconfidence. Spoiler alert: it did *not* go well. The French army got trounced in record time and Napoleon III ended up a prisoner of war, sending Eugénie (who had been left as regent in Paris) into full crisis mode. This was France's Second Empire collapsing like a badly pitched soufflé. Eugénie, running the government in her husband's absence, was soon surviving on a peculiar diet of black coffee and chloral hydrate (yes, a sedative – basically the 19th-century version of pulling all-nighters on espresso and Ambien). If that sounds like a recipe for disaster, it was. The Prussians were marching toward Paris, and internal revolution was brewing faster than Eugénie's coffee.

As the walls closed in (literally – rioters were shaking the palace gates and yelling "Down with the Spaniard!" at the Spanish-born Empress), Eugénie had to think fast. She gathered what she could of France's treasures: the Louvre's priceless art was carted off to safety, and she handed her personal jewels to a trusted confidante, Princess Pauline Metternich, who smuggled them out of the country in her diplomat husband's bag. (Who knew *diplomatic pouch* could double as the world's fanciest handbag?) Even her 14-year-old son, the Prince Imperial Louis Napoléon, was whisked away in disguise – dressed as a peasant boy and spirited over the Belgian border to save him from the revolution. It's like a twisted fairy tale: *The prince and the pauper*, except they're the same person and it's all to avoid a lynch mob.

With her family scattered and her regime in tatters, Eugénie herself slipped out of the Tuileries Palace in perhaps the most ironic getaway car ever: the private carriage of her American dentist, Dr. Thomas Evans. Yes, her knight in shining armor was a dentist from Philadelphia who realized the Empress was in danger and ushered her to safety (no novocaine needed). Dressed inconspicuously – as inconspicuously as an Empress can manage – Eugénie fled through the streets of Paris while revolutionaries were busy proclaiming a republic. If this were a movie, this is the part where the Empress, incognito in a simple dress, looks back at her burning palace and says something dramatic like, *"Well, there goes the neighborhood."* In reality, she later quipped with dark humor, "All is lost... has poor General Trochu been killed, then?" referring to the military governor who conveniently switched sides during the chaos. Gotta love a bit of sarcasm in the face of doom.

Eugénie made it out alive – first to the coastal town of Deauville and then across the English Channel to London. Britain, ever the haven for Europe's washed-up royals, welcomed the ex-Empress and eventually the released Napoleon III, who joined her after his stint as a POW. The couple reunited in exile, finding refuge in a quiet little town in Kent called Chislehurst. There, in a stately manor named Camden Place, they set up a new home that became a kind of *mini-Versailles on Thames*. The French imperial court in exile turned this sleepy English village into a bizarre imitation of France's lost glory. Imagine the scene: the French tricolor flag flutters stubbornly over the Kent countryside, and the locals suddenly have deposed royals for neighbors – it's as if someone dropped Versailles into Downton Abbey. Camden Place became "the center of the French Court in exile", complete with visits from Queen Victoria (a close friend of Eugénie) and even Tsar Alexander II of Russia. You'd see fancy carriages arriving with various European nobles coming to cheer up the Bonapartes. Diplomatic gossip sessions over tea were a regular affair, and plans to regain the French throne were fervently debated in Camden Place's drawing rooms. (Plotting a restoration while enjoying English crumpets – how very multicultural!)

Of course, the newly declared French Republic wasn't thrilled about these expat emperors scheming abroad. They even stationed spies on a nearby hill, peering at Camden Place through telescopes. Napoleon III, not one to be outwitted, had his own agents watching the watchers. It became a comedic spy vs. spy situation – think of it as a 19th-century version of *Keeping Up with the Bonapartes*, where everyone is trying to overhear everyone else. All this intrigue in a Kentish manor house! The neighbors must have been *very* confused about why their local windmill had French government agents lurking inside.

Despite the grand airs they put on, life in exile forced Eugénie and Napoleon III to simplify and show their mettle. Gone were the armies of servants (well, they still had some – old habits die hard) and the endless parade of courtiers. Instead of ruling an empire, Napoleon III took up gardening and doting on their son when he wasn't strategizing his possible comeback. Eugénie, for her part, proved to be remarkably resilient. This was no fainting damsel. She kept her dignity, hosting what courtiers remained and maintaining the *façade* of an imperial court with stiff upper lip (a very British trait she perhaps picked up). Locals in Chislehurst actually grew fond of the exiled imperial family. In 1874, when the Prince Imperial came of age at 18, the entire village threw a fête in his honor, decking out the train station in French colors and shouting *"Vive le Prince Impérial!"* like it was Bastille Day. For a brief moment, it must have felt like the empire was still alive – only relocated to suburban England.

Tragically, that moment didn't last. Fate dealt Eugénie two crushing blows: first, Napoleon III died in 1873, only a couple of years into their exile, due to complications from surgery. Eugénie was suddenly a widow, though she stoically carried on, clad in mourning black and walking the halls of Camden Place like a pint-sized Spanish Queen Victoria. Then, in 1879, disaster struck again when their beloved son, the Prince Imperial, was killed while serving in the British Army during the Anglo-Zulu War. He was only 23 and had volunteered to fight, seeking glory (or maybe just escape boredom in Kent). He died heroically (or recklessly) in a skirmish in South Africa, fighting Zulu warriors – a poignant, almost absurd end for a

Bonaparte. The people of Chislehurst lined the streets in mourning as his body was brought home, and they raised a Celtic cross memorial across from Camden Place to honor the young man who might have been Napoleon IV. It was as if the final page of the Bonaparte saga had turned, right there in their little village. Eugénie, now having lost both her empire and her only child, was heartbroken but not broken.

If you ever visit Farnborough, England, you'll find a peculiar monument to Eugénie's resilience and loyalty. After these tragedies, the Empress moved to a estate called Farnborough Hill in Hampshire, where she built a miniature abbey – a chantry chapel – to house the remains of her husband and son. This became her life's work: preserving the memory of her loved ones. She spent the next *50 years* living outside France, a dowager empress in exile, lovingly tending this mausoleum as a shrine to the Second Empire. In a sense, she turned her exile into a mission of love and remembrance. Eugénie may not have had a throne, but she *did* have a purpose. She hosted royals and friends at Farnborough (Queen Victoria remained a dear friend who often visited for tea and commiseration – imagine those conversations: one empress sans empire, and one queen who once called herself "Mrs. Brown" sneaking off to Scotland – they had a lot to talk about).

At Farnborough Hill, Eugénie curated a veritable museum of her life – furnishing the house with portraits, furniture, and tapestries rescued from the Tuileries and other imperial residences, even fighting the French government for their return. Walking into her home was like stepping into a time capsule of the Second Empire: Winterhalter portraits on the walls, Napoleonic bees and eagles on the décor, and a sense that this exiled empress was *determined* to keep her identity alive. She once feared ending up like Marie Antoinette (guillotine and all), but her fate was different: a long, quiet life in England, defined not by tragedy alone, but by steadfastness and even a certain grace in survival.

Eugénie died in 1920 at the ripe age of 94 – outliving Napoleon III by nearly 50 years and witnessing a new era (she even allegedly took a ride in an airplane and met young Winston Churchill in her later years – talk about *staying relevant*). The French certainly took note of her endurance; one could say she had the last laugh, living long enough to see France go through multiple republics and crises while she maintained her imperial dignity abroad. Her story shows us that loyalty and love can endure even when titles and riches are stripped away. She never stopped being "Empress Eugénie" in her heart, but she also proved her worth as Eugénie *the survivor*. In exile, without a palace or subjects, she revealed character traits that ruling in luxury might have kept hidden: courage, compassion, and a touch of witty resilience. As she preserved the legacy of the Bonapartes, she also forged her own legacy – one of unbroken love and loyalty. And as we leave her story, one can't help but imagine Eugénie in heaven, sipping coffee (no chloral hydrate needed this time) and chuckling that a dentist and a little English hospitality saved the last Empress of the French.

Our next tale takes us from 19th-century England to the late 20th century, proving that exiled royals and their comebacks aren't just a Victorian melodrama. Buckle up (or, rather, tighten your crown): we're heading to the Balkans, where a boy king named Simeon will show the world that sometimes you can go home again – even if you have to win an election to do it.

The Boy Who Would Be Prime Minister: Simeon of Bulgaria's Comeback

Tsar Simeon II as a child in the 1940s – a little boy in a big royal uniform. He would later trade his epaulets for a business suit and a ballot box.

In a plot twist that sounds straight out of a Hollywood dramedy, King Simeon II of Bulgaria went from being a child monarch to an exiled schoolboy, then decades later to a democratically elected Prime Minister of his country. Yes, you read that right – it's like if the kid from *Home Alone* grew up and won the presidency. Simeon's saga is a crash course in resilience and adapting to wildly changing circumstances, with a healthy dose of *"You can't make this stuff up."*

Our story begins in Bulgaria during World War II. Simeon was born in 1937 as a prince of the Bulgarian royal family (full name: Simeon Borisov Saxe-Coburg-Gotha – a surname about as long as a Bulgarian winter). In 1943, at the tender age of six, he unexpectedly became Tsar Simeon II after his father, Tsar Boris III, died suddenly. Imagine *Play-Doh* in one hand and the burden of a kingdom in the other. Of course, a toddler king isn't calling the shots – a regency council took over the actual governing while little Simeon learned how to write his name (probably easier than learning to spell "Saxe-Coburg-Gotha"). For a few years, he was a living symbol of the monarchy, trotted out for ceremonies in a tiny uniform that made dignitaries go "aww."

But post-war Eastern Europe was no fairy tale for royals. In 1946, as the Iron Curtain spread, Bulgaria's new Communist authorities decided they had no room for a monarchy. They held a referendum which (surprise!) voted to abolish the monarchy – historical accounts suggest the vote might have been, shall we say, *strongly encouraged* by those in power. The result was swift and irreversible: 9-year-old Simeon was dethroned and sent packing. One day he's King, the next he's essentially stateless. The royal family fled into exile, narrowly escaping what could have been a much worse fate if they'd stayed. It was a traumatic upheaval – try explaining to a second-grader why he's got to leave his home because a referendum said so. Simeon and his sister and mother first found refuge in Egypt (the young King Farouk of Egypt was a cousin, conveniently). Later they settled in Spain, where the Franco regime – not a fan of communists, to say the least – welcomed them. Thus began Simeon's new life as plain Simeon Sakskoourggotski, the kid in exile.

For the next half-century, Simeon lived as far from a king's life as you can imagine. Picture a royal living in Madrid, growing up in the care of a former king-turned-dad who now has to figure out school enrollments and grocery shopping. It's a bit like a real-life *Coming to America*, except he *left* home royalty and arrived as a nobody. He went to school (a military academy in Spain, then law and business studies – no lounging in palaces for this guy), and he learned Spanish and the art of being incognito. In exile, Simeon married a Spanish aristocrat, Doña Margarita, in 1962, and they started a family.

By all accounts, he became a successful businessman – the once-upon-a-time boy king morphing into a suited executive. If you met him in the 1980s, you might think he was just another well-heeled Madrid gentleman with a secret: *"Oh by the way, I used to be the King of Bulgaria. Pass the salt, please."* No kingdom, no crown, but a stable family life and career – talk about redefining royal priorities. His love for Bulgaria, however, never dimmed. He reportedly kept in touch with Bulgarian culture and events from afar, quietly nurturing the hope that he might one day return.

That day came in the 1990s with the fall of communism. As Eastern Europe's regimes toppled like dominoes, exiled royals suddenly found themselves back in style (or at least, back in the news). In 1996, after 50 years in exile, Simeon II set foot in Bulgaria again. He was greeted by massive crowds and a *"rapturous welcome"* in Sofia. Imagine the scene: the now late-middle-aged Simeon (he was nearly 60) arriving to throngs waving flags and crying tears of joy. Many Bulgarians had no memory of him as King – he was, after all, a child last time they saw him – but the very idea of a link to pre-communist Bulgaria was enough to cause excitement. Here was a man who had literally been a *Disney prince in exile*, returning to the kingdom like a character who stepped out of a time machine. It didn't matter that he came back not in a golden carriage but on a standard commercial flight (in economy class, he joked, next to a tourist with a chicken – okay, I made up the chicken, but the point is he came back humbly). The symbolism was huge.

What Simeon did next shocked everyone. He didn't campaign to restore the monarchy or start living in a castle (though a family estate, Vrana Palace, was returned to him and he did spend his first night there, soaking in nostalgia). Instead, he listened to the people – who, while fond of him, had no appetite for undoing decades of republican government – and he chose a different path. In 2001, Simeon did something arguably even more extraordinary than reclaiming a throne: he ran for office in a democracy. That's right, the former king formed a political party (cheekily named the "National Movement

Simeon II" as if to remind voters *hey, remember me?*) and promised to bring prosperity and clean governance. The Bulgarians, dealing with post-communist economic woes, decided to take a chance on him. In a sweeping victory, Simeon's party won the most seats in parliament. The ex-king was soon invited to form a government and became Prime Minister Simeon Saxe-Coburg-Gotha (or "Mr. Saxe-Coburg," as newspapers dubbed him for simplicity). He thus earned the unique distinction of being *the first exiled monarch in Eastern Europe to regain political power through the ballot box*. Who needs a coronation when you have a mandate from the people?

To appreciate how wild this is: imagine if someone like *Prince Harry* decades from now ran for Prime Minister of a country and won – it was that surreal. Yet, to Bulgarians, Simeon's return felt less like a celebrity stunt and more like poetic justice. Here was a man who had every excuse to turn bitter or distance himself, but instead he came back home to help when it mattered. And the loyalty wasn't one-sided: though Bulgarians didn't want the crown back (they'd grown used to the idea of a republic), they held Simeon in high regard, admiring his aristocratic air and success as a businessman. He polled as one of the most popular public figures in the country, topping approval charts at around 74%. Not bad for someone whose previous political experience was, well, being born royal.

Simeon's term as Prime Minister (2001–2005) had its ups and downs – governing is a lot harder than cutting ribbons as a ceremonial king. He pursued economic reforms and led Bulgaria toward joining the EU and NATO, emphasizing that his focus was on the people's well-being, not any royal restoration. In fact, he explicitly ruled out any attempt to reclaim the throne, pledging allegiance to the republican constitution just like any other office-holder. Picture the scene at his swearing-in: the former Tsar in a suit, hand on the Bible, promising to uphold the republic – the irony could not have been richer. It's as if a former quarterback returned to coach the team, but first had to promise not to put on a helmet again. There's a certain humility and wisdom in that. Simeon understood that leadership isn't about titles; it's about service. He famously announced he would "make a difference in 800 days" – a rather specific promise that commentators joked sounded like a warranty period. Whether he achieved that is up for debate, but Bulgaria did see improvements and eventually joined the European Union shortly after his tenure, which was one of his government's big goals.

Throughout all this, Margarita, his wife, was a stalwart partner. The two presented a picture of stability and unity – no tabloid scandals, no extravagance. By all accounts, Margarita (who became *Tsaritsa* in title after their marriage, and later simply the Prime Minister's wife) adapted to her husband's homeland with grace, even learning Bulgarian. The love that kept them together through long years of exile now played out on the public stage, as they navigated formal state dinners instead of just private family dinners. It's almost sitcom-worthy: *"My husband the King... is now my husband the Prime Minister!"* (Laugh track here). Yet they handled it with dignity and a pinch of humor – Simeon was often seen smiling, perhaps at the absurdity of his own journey.

After leaving office in 2005, Simeon eventually retired from politics when his party's fortunes waned. Today, he remains an elder statesman figure – one of the very few people *in the world* who can say they've been both a king and an elected head of government. (Fun fact: As of 2025, Simeon II and the Dalai Lama are the only two living people who were heads of state during WWII – and both had mostly symbolic roles back then. History has a strange sense of humor.) Simeon's life illustrates that true nobility isn't about sitting on a throne; it's about how you handle life when the throne is taken away. In exile, he didn't wallow or scheme vainly; he educated himself, built a career, and kept his love for his country alive. When the opportunity came, he returned not as a king demanding a crown, but as a citizen offering to serve. Loyalty? He had it in spades – loyalty to Bulgaria's people and to the idea that he could help them, crown or no crown. Resilience? Absolutely – from a displaced child to a savvy leader, he adapted to every twist of fate. And underlying it all, a kind of quiet love – for his heritage, for the family that stood by him, and for the country that welcomed him home in the end.

It's a story so incredible that if it weren't true, you'd think it was a quirky Netflix series. (In fact, somebody please pitch this: *"Banished King, Bulgarian Edition"*, complete with a training montage of Simeon studying for his citizenship exam – except he never lost his Bulgarian citizenship technically, but you get the idea.) Simeon's tale links nicely with our other stories by showing that whether you're an empress in a British exile or a king without a country, it's what you do in the aftermath that counts. From Simeon, we learn that character is destiny. When life knocked him down, he got back up – not in the way he or anyone originally expected, but in a way that was perhaps even more meaningful.

Now, for our final stop, we turn to a royal couple whose exile was a joint venture: King Constantine II of Greece and his wife, Queen Anne-Marie. Their journey takes us through palace coups,

Mediterranean odysseys (literally, given all the countries they lived in), and an eventual homecoming that ties a poignant bow on the theme of enduring love. If you thought being a solo ex-monarch was hard, try doing it as a young married couple with babies in tow. It's time to see how *two* hearts, united by marriage and tested by exile, remained unbroken through it all.

A Crownless King and His Queen: Constantine II & Anne-Marie's Odyssey

In the annals of exiled royals, King Constantine II of Greece and Queen Anne-Marie deserve a chapter all their own. Their story has all the elements of a modern epic – a dash of *Game of Thrones*-style upheaval (minus the dragons), a bit of *The Crown* (young attractive royals, political drama), and a lot of real-life *Odyssey*, as they wandered for almost half a century away from their homeland. Through it all, one thing remained constant (pardon the pun): their dedication to each other and to the idea of one day returning home, not as monarchs with pomp and circumstance, but as husband and wife with a truly tested love.

Let's set the scene: It's the mid-1960s in Greece, and young King Constantine II is the new monarch – dashing, athletic, even an Olympic gold medalist in sailing from the 1960 Rome Games. (Yes, this king literally had *sporting medals* as well as royal ones). In 1964, at age 24, he married Princess Anne-Marie of Denmark, who was just 18 and absolutely radiant – imagine a wedding straight out of a storybook, with royals from all over Europe attending. Anne-Marie herself was a Danish princess (and, fun fact, the younger sister of Denmark's current Queen Margrethe II), so this union was like a pan-

European alliance of youthful charm. Greek crowds adored the royal couple; they were glamorous, like the William and Kate of their day, always smiling and bringing a bit of Nordic cool to the Mediterranean heat. But, as every viewer of *The Crown* knows, the 1960s were a turbulent time for monarchies. Greece was no exception – in fact, it was worse than most.

In 1967, only a few years after their fairy-tale wedding, Constantine and Anne-Marie's world was turned upside down. A group of Greek military colonels staged a coup d'état (the infamous "Colonels' coup") and seized control of the government. Constantine was only 26, and suddenly he was facing a national crisis that seasoned politicians would have struggled with. Initially, he tried to work with the new junta, swearing them in (likely while gritting his teeth) in hopes of preserving the monarchy. But dictatorships and kings don't mix well; by December of that year, Constantine attempted a counter-coup to restore democracy – a bold move, but it failed due to lack of sufficient military support. Realizing the jig was up, Constantine, Anne-Marie, and their two small children (they had a one-year-old baby and Anne-Marie was pregnant with their third at the time – timing couldn't have been worse) fled Greece for their lives on 13 December 1967. They barely had time to pack. Famously, Anne-Marie left in such haste that she didn't even grab a coat, braving the winter air in an evening gown – talk about a dramatic exit. The young family escaped by plane to Rome, Italy, suddenly finding themselves royals without a realm.

Thus began an exile that would last 46 years. Think about that – they left as a couple in their twenties and would not live in Greece again until they were senior citizens. At first, they thought it might be temporary. Constantine steadfastly refused to abdicate, hoping for a reversal of fortunes. For a few years he styled himself as the king-in-exile, maintaining formalities and communicating with supporters back home. The Greek junta, however, abolished the monarchy in 1973, and a referendum in 1974 after the junta's fall sealed the deal – Greece became firmly a republic. Constantine was officially deposed and even stripped of his Greek citizenship in 1994 by a socialist government upset over a property dispute. (That's right: the king who once reigned over the land couldn't even call himself a citizen of it – *bureaucracy has a cruel sense of humor.*) During those decades, the exiled King and Queen lived mainly in London, with stints in Rome and Copenhagen (the Danish royal family gave them a refuge for a while too – perks of having in-laws with palaces). In London, they eventually settled in a suburban house in Hampstead Garden Suburb, a far cry from the marble halls of Athens. Neighbors would see Constantine mowing his lawn or going for a stroll, looking every bit the affable, balding middle-aged man next door – albeit one who might casually mention his *cousin Elizabeth at Buckingham Palace* or his *godson Prince William.* (Yes, they were *that* well-connected: Constantine was Prince William's godfather, and Prince Philip was Constantine's first cousin. European royalty is one very tangled family tree.)

For Anne-Marie, the exile meant adapting from being "Her Majesty the Queen of the Hellenes" to being a mother, wife, and private citizen in a foreign country. By all accounts, she did so with remarkable grace. She and Constantine raised five children during their exile – three of whom were born in London, never knowing what it was like to live in their royal homeland. Imagine telling bedtime stories about *"when we were in the palace"* to kids who only know you as Mom and Dad in a normal house. Anne-Marie kept the family tightly knit, instilling in her children a love for Greece and their heritage even though they grew up in England. She was the emotional rock of the family – the powerful matriarch in the background, ensuring that exile didn't equal misery. Of course, they had their struggles.

At one point, the Greek government seized Tatoi Palace (their former residence in Athens) and other royal properties, leading Constantine to fight a long legal battle that ended with a minimal compensation. They also had the odd challenge of last names – Greek authorities insisted that if Constantine wanted a passport, he needed a surname like everyone else (Greek royals traditionally didn't use one). The press had a field day with that: *"Former King needs last name – suggestions welcome!"* (He eventually traveled on a Danish passport under the name "Constantine de Grecia," which literally means "Constantine of Greece" – a little on the nose, right?). Through all this, Anne-Marie stood by him, often literally holding his hand at public events where they were still called King and Queen by courtesy. They might not have had a throne, but they had each other, and that seemed to be enough.

Despite being out of power, Constantine never truly gave up on Greece. He kept in touch with Greek affairs from afar and was reportedly *homesick* to the core. When Greece went through the devastating economic crisis in the 2010s, something unexpected happened: Constantine and Anne-Marie decided it was finally time to go *home*. In 2013, with Greece in financial turmoil and many Greeks emigrating for better opportunities, the exiled king and queen quietly moved back to Athens. The timing raised a few eyebrows (some joked, "Trust a king to show up when real estate prices hit rock bottom!"). In fact, there's truth in that jest: they had just sold their London house for a tidy £9.5 million, and Athens property was dirt cheap due to the crisis, so downsizing in Greece made economic sense. But it wasn't just about the money. Constantine was 73 by then, and he frankly said he didn't want to die in exile. Greece was his birthplace, his identity. And so, the couple came back not to a palace (those were long gone) but to a relatively modest home in Athens. The news stunned Greeks – many of whom had never expected to see the former royal family living among them again. Reactions were mixed: older folks who remembered the monarchy had a nostalgia trip, royalists rejoiced, but republicans side-eyed this development with suspicion. Constantine promised he had no political ambitions, and indeed he mostly kept a low profile, seen occasionally in public with a cane, greeting acquaintances and old friends. Anne-Marie engaged in quiet charity work and finally could enjoy her "beloved country" again – she had been barred from even visiting Greece for years, except once in 1981 to attend her mother-in-law's funeral. Now she could walk the streets of Athens freely, a Greek queen without a crown but with her dignity intact.

The true test of their love and character had lasted decades, and they aced it. They celebrated anniversaries far from the land where they'd wed, yet their bond only grew. If gossip columns were hoping for sensational fights or royal divorce drama, they were disappointed – Constantine and Anne-Marie were solid. One could argue that losing their official roles early on allowed them to focus on what truly mattered: family and personal integrity. When you've gone from ruling a country to fretting over your kids' school grades and paying the heating bill in an English winter, you learn humility in a hurry. Constantine had been a king, yes, but exile taught him to be a regular man too.

Anne-Marie had been a queen, but exile made her a steadfast partner and mother, navigating everything from learning new languages to cooking dinner (rumor has it she makes a mean moussaka, though with Danish meatballs on the side). They carried on royal traditions in small ways – for example, the family still used royal titles among themselves and in the European royal circuit, which occasionally led to awkward moments like, "Your Majesty – uh, I mean, Mr. de Grecia – could you sign here, please?" But they also embraced normalcy. Their children grew up relatively down-to-earth; one son even worked as a financier, one daughter as an actress in London. It wasn't exactly *The Simple Life*, but compared to palace living, it was modest.

Finally, in January 2023, after a long life that could fill several memoirs, Constantine II passed away in Athens at age 82. In a touching full-circle moment, he died not in exile but back in his homeland, with Anne-Marie and their children by his side. At his funeral (a private service, since officially he was just a "former King" being buried as a citizen), dignitaries and blue-bloods from all over Europe flew in – a testament to the royal family ties Anne-Marie especially had kept up. But the most poignant sight was Queen Anne-Marie herself, paying tribute to her beloved husband in a deeply symbolic way. She wore the same crucifix she had worn on their wedding day, and in her hair she wore a wreath of white lilies – the very same type of flowers that adorned her bridal bouquet in 1964. In that subtle homage, Anne-Marie sent a powerful message: that through all the upheaval, the heart of their story was a marriage built on love and loyalty from beginning to end. She had been a teenager in a tiara, saying "I do" to a dashing young king, and nearly 59 years later, she said goodbye to him with the symbols of that very union. There wasn't a dry eye among those who understood the significance. It was the closing of a chapter – not just for a man who once was king, but for a love that had weathered exile's storms and never faltered.

The tale of Constantine and Anne-Marie underscores something profound: true character is revealed in survival, not in luxury. When they had a palace, guards, and the whole country bowing to them, who could really tell what they were made of? It was when all that was stripped away – when they were loading luggage into a station wagon in Rome, or hosting friends in a modest London living room, or apartment-hunting in Athens at age 70 – that we saw their true colors. And those colors were solid gold (figuratively speaking; literally, they pawned a lot of the gold to keep afloat!). They remained kind, devoted, and hopeful. They didn't scheme to reclaim power by force or wallow in bitterness. Instead, they focused on their roles as husband and wife, parents and eventually grandparents, and quietly on being good neighbors and citizens wherever they lived. One might say they lived the idea that love and loyalty are portable – you can take them with you no matter where you go, no crown required.

Conclusion: Loyalty Beyond Thrones

Bringing together these three stories – Eugénie and Napoleon III, Simeon II of Bulgaria, Constantine II and Anne-Marie of Greece – we find a unifying moral worthy of a royal crest: *"Fortune's wheel can toss you down, but true character will lift you back up."* In each case, the gilded trappings of monarchy fell away, and our protagonists had to continue life as mere mortals with extraordinary backstories. And in each case, they demonstrated that the essence of royalty isn't in the crown on one's head but in the heart beating beneath the ermine and velvet.

- Loyalty: Empress Eugénie, bereft of her empire, remained fiercely loyal to her husband's memory and her son's legacy. She spent half a century guarding their honor in a foreign land. King Simeon stayed loyal to his people, returning not as a ruler by right but as a servant by choice, earning the respect of a new generation. King Constantine and Queen Anne-Marie epitomized loyalty to each other – sticking together through exile's indignities and never giving up on the dream of going home.

- Resilience: These royals-turned-refugees showed an almost stubborn toughness. They adapted – whether it was Eugénie turning an English estate into a little piece of France, Simeon reinventing himself as a modern politician, or Constantine learning to navigate London's public transport (okay, maybe he had a driver, but you get the idea). They endured personal losses, culture shocks, and years of uncertainty. And when new opportunities arose – be it a chance to influence national affairs again, or a chance to quietly reclaim their place in their homeland – they seized them with both hands.

- Love Outside the Palace Walls: Perhaps most strikingly, when the pomp and protocol were stripped away, these individuals leaned on love – the love of spouses, of family, of country.

Without throne rooms to sit in, they sat at family dinner tables. Without court ceremonies, they celebrated personal milestones in intimate gatherings. And those bonds proved unbreakable. It's easy to pledge love "for better or worse" in a cathedral packed with cheering subjects; it's another thing to live that vow in a two-bedroom flat in a foreign city. Yet that's exactly what Constantine and Anne-Marie did. It's easy for a leader to say they love their country; it's another to come back without a title, just to help, as Simeon did. It's easy to love the *idea* of being an empress; harder to love the life of an exile – but Eugénie found purpose even in that, powered by love for those she lost.

And let's not forget the *humor* and humanity that peeked through these stories. We have an empress saved by a dentist (no royal protocol for cavity-filling escapes), a king who had to campaign like a regular guy and got called "Mr. Coburg" by the press, and a queen who probably had to ask her neighbor in London how to operate the washing machine. These little anecdotes and imagined scenes aren't just comic relief – they remind us that stripped of titles, these people were, well, people. They had to learn, adapt, sometimes laugh at themselves, and carry on. In doing so, they arguably became more admirable than they were on their thrones. They turned misfortune into a character test, and they passed with flying colors (royal blue and gold, presumably).

In a world often obsessed with power and success, the lives of Eugénie, Simeon, Constantine, and Anne-Marie tell a different tale: the true measure of a person – royal or not – is how they handle loss and adversity. Each of them discovered that the greatest crown one can wear is not made of gold and gems, but of integrity, resilience, and love. Palaces crumble, thrones are lost, titles fade, but the way you treat those you love, and the way you face hardships, those leave a legacy no revolution can erase.

So, *Love in Exile – Banished, But Not Broken* is more than a catchy chapter title. It's a salute to all who find themselves in unwelcome new circumstances and refuse to be defined by them. It's a wink to the idea that sometimes you have to lose it all to find out what you really have. And it's a gentle reminder – with a smile and a wink – that history isn't just made by those who wield power in the limelight, but also by those who live nobly in the shadows. After all, as these stories show, a royal at heart remains royal in spirit, with or without a kingdom. And that is a legacy of love and strength that truly endures.

Chapter 8

Cross-Cultural Unions –
When Borders Blur for Love

Love has a cheeky habit of laughing in the face of borders. Throughout history, Cupid's arrows have flitted across continents and cultures with little regard for the rules of kings, customs, or common sense. The result? Some truly spectacular cross-cultural love stories that left the world gasping, gossiping, and occasionally applauding in delight. In this chapter, we journey through three such romances – tales where Hollywood royalty crashes into actual royalty, where a king swaps formal statecraft for the art of wooing an American, and where colonial-era star-crossed lovers defy imperial decorum. Each story brims with culture clash and transformation, with the lovers serving as brave ambassadors to each other's worlds. And yes, the media of their day ate it all up like it was the last piece of cake at a royal wedding. Through witty storytelling and a pinch of satire, we'll see how these unions symbolized more than just starry-eyed affection – they showcased the power of respect, curiosity, and adaptation across cultural divides.

So, grab some popcorn (or perhaps a cup of tea with a dash of curry) and settle in. Our first stop is the sunny Riviera in the 1950s, where an American film starlet found that the role of her life wasn't on a soundstage at all – it was in the gilded halls of a small European principality.

Grace Kelly and Prince Rainier: A Hollywood Fairytale in Monaco

Prince Rainier III of Monaco and Grace Kelly arriving at the White House in 1961, five years after their celebrated "wedding of the century." Once upon a time – 1955, to be precise – a Hollywood starlet met a real-life prince. Grace Kelly was at the Cannes Film Festival when she was introduced to Prince Rainier III of Monaco. Sparks flew (politely), and a transatlantic courtship blossomed. Less than a year later, Rainier proposed and Grace accepted – an actress was about to become a princess.

The engagement announcement sent reporters into a frenzy. It was the first time a Hollywood star had infiltrated the ranks of a royal family, and the story was irresistible: a movie star pairing off with the playboy prince of a postcard-perfect kingdom. Media on both sides of the Atlantic devoured the news like a decadent dessert, splashing the couple's photos and every tidbit of gossip across front pages. Grace and Rainier were described as a match made in publicity heaven – the glamorous film goddess and the eligible prince of a tiny principality was incredible fodder for newspapers worldwide. Never mind that Monaco was smaller than some Hollywood backlots; for the press this was a real-life Cinderella story. In today's terms, it was like an A-list celebrity marrying a European prince – a transatlantic power couple that prefigured Meghan and Harry by decades.

The royal wedding in April 1956 was a spectacle for the ages. Monaco hosted a civil ceremony followed the next day by a grand church service. Hollywood's MGM studios even filmed it – over 30 million people watched on live television around the world, transfixed by this real-life fairytale. Grace's bridal gown (a gift from MGM's wardrobe department) and the star-studded guest list made headlines, and the event has been called the first modern example of global media overkill. In short, it was the "wedding of the century," and everyone wanted a glimpse of the American actress-turned-princess.

Grace gave up her acting career at 26 to become Princess of Monaco. Stepping off the soundstage and into a palace wasn't all smooth sailing – she learned French, mastered royal protocol, and even curtsied to her own husband at times. Yet Grace poured herself into charitable work and cultural initiatives, leveraging her Hollywood glamour for the good of Monaco. Over time, her genuine dedication won over any skeptics. By all accounts, their marriage was strong – Rainier and Grace shared a deep mutual respect and affection that helped bridge their very different worlds. They raised three children and remained devoted until Grace's tragic death in 1982, a finale that shook the principality and the wider world.

King Hussein and Queen Noor: An Arabian King and His All-American Queen

King Hussein of Jordan and Queen Noor (born Lisa Halaby) during a state visit in 1978, not long after their cross-cultural royal wedding.

Fast forward to the late 1970s in the Middle East, where another royal met an unlikely American bride. If Grace's story was a Hollywood fairytale, Hussein and Noor's was more like a modern epic – part romance, part diplomatic drama. King Hussein of Jordan – widowed and in search of a partner – crossed paths with Lisa Najeeb Halaby in 1977. Lisa was a Princeton-educated Arab-American working in Amman on aviation projects, and their connection was instant. Within a year, Hussein proposed, and Lisa accepted; she converted to Islam and took the name Noor al-Hussein, meaning "Light of Hussein". In June 1978 they married in a traditional ceremony at the palace in Amman, making her the first American-born queen of an Arab country.

Becoming Queen Noor required major adaptation. She learned Arabic, embraced Jordanian customs, and even took on the care of Hussein's children from previous marriages. At first, some Jordanians were wary of a foreign-born queen, wondering if she would understand their ways. But Noor's sincere dedication – and her own Arab roots (her father's family was originally from Syria) – endeared her to the public over time. She championed education, women's rights, and urban planning in Jordan, quickly proving she was more than a photogenic consort.

Hussein, a modern-minded monarch, proudly gave his wife the title of "Queen" (not merely princess consort) upon marriage, signaling their partnership. The couple became a formidable team on the world stage, with Queen Noor often by the King's side in diplomatic events. Their marriage was warm and grounded in mutual respect – a true meeting of East and West under one roof. Over two decades, King Hussein and Queen Noor showed that love, curiosity, and respect could bridge the gap between an American upbringing and a Jordanian throne. When Hussein died in 1999, Jordanians lauded Noor not as an outsider, but as a beloved queen mother figure who had brought new light to their kingdom.

Indian Maharanis and British Officers: Love in the Time of the Raj

A late-18th-century portrait by Johann Zoffany depicting Major William Palmer, an officer of the East India Company, with his Mughal princess wife and extended family in India. Such images captured the unlikely unions that occurred when imperial duty met love.

Long before transoceanic royal weddings were being broadcast on TV, the British Raj in India produced its own genre of cross-cultural romance – albeit usually without the fairytale fanfare and often with a lot more scandal. In the 19th-century British Empire, the social rule was clear: the English ruling class and the Indian princely class were not meant to mix as equals, let alone marry. But love, that irrepressible troublemaker, found ways to defy the strict social order. Every so often, a stiff-upper-lipped British officer and an elegant Indian princess (a Maharani) would strike up an acquaintance that blossomed into something that gave the Viceroy heartburn.

These romances were usually the stuff of whispers in the clubhouses of Calcutta and the drawing rooms of London. Imagine a Victorian-era gossip column: *"Dear me, have you heard? Major So-and-So has gone and married the Maharajah's daughter!"* Monocles would drop into teacups; fans would flutter anxiously. It wasn't *supposed* to happen – but happen it did. In fact, back in the late 18th century, during the East India Company days, such unions were not as rare as later Victorian society might suggest. The wills of that period show that by the 1780s, over one-third of British men in India were leaving all their possessions to one or more Indian wives. Yes, astonishing as it sounds, many early colonizers "went native" in matters of the heart, taking local wives and adopting local ways.

Take Colonel William Gardner, for instance – an English officer who fell in love with a Mughal princess and converted to Islam to marry her in 1796. He left the British army and made a life in India as the husband of his Begum, a decision that raised many an eyebrow among his countrymen. Another bold romantic was James Achilles Kirkpatrick, a British Resident in Hyderabad who secretly wed Khair-un-Nissa, a teenaged noblewoman, in a private Muslim ceremony. Kirkpatrick donned Persian attire and embraced local customs, scandalizing the colonial establishment when word of this interracial union leaked out. Such *White Mughal* romances were rare but very real – moments when personal passion trumped the racial barriers of empire.

Life for these cross-cultural couples in the Raj was not easy. If they stayed in India, they often faced social ostracism from the British side – no more invitations to the officer's club, and polite society might pointedly "forget" to call on a fellow who had taken an Indian wife. The Indian side could be equally unwelcoming; a Maharani who married a foreigner risked displeasing her royal relatives or even being disowned from her palace. If the couple went to Britain, the culture shock was immense. The Indian bride exchanged her saris for corseted Victorian gowns and struggled with English weather (trading monsoons for months of drizzle). She encountered prejudice in a society that viewed her as a curiosity at best. Some adapted brilliantly – imagine a former Indian princess hosting afternoon tea in a Yorkshire manor, serving cucumber sandwiches alongside samosas, quietly bemusing her neighbors. Others struggled, feeling neither here nor there. But those who made it work did so through an abundance of respect and curiosity for each other's backgrounds. In their private sphere, they created a fusion of two worlds: perhaps celebrating Diwali and Christmas, or blending curries and roast beef at dinner. By simply living and loving together, they were thumbing their noses at the notion that East and West could never meet.

Interestingly, not all such stories ended in scandal or isolation. In some cases, these unions helped soften relations between communities. A British officer who genuinely respected his Indian wife's culture might become a more empathetic liaison with local rulers. Likewise, an Indian princess who married an Englishman could humanize the "foreign rulers" in the eyes of her people – *he* wasn't just a conqueror, he was family. These were the exceptions rather than the rule, but they hinted at what was possible when mutual understanding prevailed.

As the sun set on the British Raj in 1947, many of these mixed families faced new dilemmas. Some British officers chose to remain in the newly independent India or Pakistan with their Indian wives, becoming part of the fabric of those nations. Others relocated to England, where their children grew up navigating hyphenated identities (and sometimes amusing their classmates with stories of their Maharani grandmothers). The legacy of these unions lived on in those children and grandchildren – living proof that the dividing lines of empire were not as impermeable as they seemed.

If all this sounds terribly romantic, it certainly had its dramatic side. It's the kind of thing that makes historians smile and racists frown. As one commentator quipped, the British went to India to conquer, but some ended up *surrendering* – to love.

Conclusion: When Love Bridges Worlds

In these stories of cross-cultural unions, we find more than tabloid fascination or fairy-tale escapism. We find lessons about what it takes for love to bridge worlds. First and foremost, it takes respect – genuine, roll-up-your-sleeves respect for your partner's background, be it a different faith, a different language, or just a different way of dancing at weddings. Grace Kelly embraced Monaco's traditions, learning the language and the etiquette; Prince Rainier welcomed her American openness and Hollywood flair. Queen Noor immersed herself in Jordanian life and Arabic language, while King Hussein valued her independent spirit and ideas. The British-Indian couples of the Raj who made it work did so by honoring each other's customs – sometimes against all odds. They proved, in their intimate sphere, what skeptical pundits often deny in the political sphere: that East and West can meet and enrich one another. As one historian noted, such romances remind us that it is entirely possible to reconcile two worlds – it's only prejudice and fear that keep them apart.

Secondly, these love stories thrived on curiosity and adaptability. The people involved didn't cling rigidly to their own way of life; instead, they leaned in to learn about the other's. Grace swapped Hollywood banter for French phrases and discovered a new sense of purpose beyond the silver screen. Noor adopted the role of an Arab queen and used it to champion causes in a land foreign to her birthplace. The British officers who "went native" in India – learning Urdu, wearing local dress, partaking in local festivals – might have scandalized their peers, but they built bridges within their marriages that transcended empires. Each couple, in essence, created a tiny model of what global harmony could look like, with a foot in each world and hearts in the middle.

And what of the outside world looking in? The fascination has always been there. We're drawn to these stories because they're hopeful. They suggest that maybe, just maybe, humanity isn't hopelessly divided into clashing civilizations destined never to understand each other. Instead, they show that when individuals reach across the divide, others follow. Grace and Rainier's union captivated people who suddenly saw transatlantic kinship where before there was an ocean. Hussein and Noor's partnership sent a message that tradition and modernity could coexist in the Middle East, inspiring young women across the region to pursue education and public service. The quiet, daring marriages in the Raj era challenged the racist norms of their time and foreshadowed the multicultural societies of the future. Children of such unions often grew up to be bridge-builders themselves, fluent in both their heritages and comfortable in a world of mixed identities.

Of course, love alone didn't erase all challenges. Each couple faced skeptics and obstacles. But by sticking together and carving out a shared identity, they made it work. They turned "us and them" into *us, together.* And that might be the most powerful takeaway: through genuine respect, curiosity, and a dash of humor, love can transform a union of two people into a union of two cultures.

So, what's the moral of this globe-trotting, time-hopping tale? Simply that love can bridge worlds when mutual respect thrives. It's not about one side yielding to the other; it's about both sides bending toward each other, meeting in the middle. In a world often obsessed with differences, these couples teach us to find the common song and dance to it – even if one partner is doing the waltz and the other the bhangra at first, eventually they create a rhythm uniquely their own.

Perhaps the best ambassadors aren't always the ones in suits at the United Nations, but the ones in wedding attire saying "I do" across cultural lines. In their private hearts, they do the work of diplomacy every day, showing that borders truly blur for love. And as we toast to these extraordinary couples (with champagne, or chai, or coffee – take your pick), we're reminded that when hearts are open and respect is mutual, love can indeed leap over any wall, climb any palace gate, and bridge any border. Cheers to love, the greatest world traveler of all.

Chapter 9

Same-Sex Secrets –
Hidden Loves Behind the Throne

Royal life has always had an ironic flair: while Monarchs parade in public under strict tradition, behind palace doors they sometimes defy those very norms in the most human ways. History is peppered with rulers whose same-sex secrets simmered behind thrones draped in velvet. In this chapter, we embark on a witty romp through three such stories – spanning from a king's *bromance* in 17th-century England to a cross-dressing Habsburg archduke in the 19th century, and finally a modern royal who said "I do" to his male love in a very 21st-century way. Each tale blends secrecy, repression, and (eventually) liberation, proving that even under crowns and coronets, the heart wants what it wants. Through humorous storytelling and satirical asides, we'll see how these hidden (or not-so-hidden) royal romances speak volumes about identity, social norms, and the slow march toward openness. After all, truth, however concealed, *longs for light* – and honesty, in the end, outlasts even the stodgiest old traditions.

King James I & Duke of Buckingham – A Jacobean Bromance

A 17th-century court portrait captures the lavish style of a royal favorite resplendent in satin and lace, projecting an image of virtue while whispering secrets might have swirled behind those confident eyes.

Let's travel back to the early 1600s, where we find King James I of England (also James VI of Scotland) making waves with an intimate royal *friendship* that had all of London's gossip mills churning. The king was known for having "favorites" – handsome young men upon whom he heaped titles, gifts, and unabashed affection. Chief among them was George Villiers, the Duke of Buckingham, a charismatic man twenty years the king's junior who rocketed from minor gentry to ducal eminence at lightning speed. How? Well, *love* (or something like it) works faster than a royal messenger hawk. By 1615, James had plucked Villiers from obscurity and made him Gentleman of the Bedchamber, kicking off one of history's most notorious royal bromances.

Contemporaries noticed there was *something more* than political mentorship brewing. James was a king who didn't hide his affection well – he literally could not get enough of Buckingham. One Venetian ambassador reported (in what might be the 17th-century equivalent of a tabloid scoop) that James "will not eat, sup or remain an hour without him and considers him his whole joy". The King spent *all his time* with Buckingham, leaning on his shoulder at court, showering him with kisses in public, and generally acting like a smitten schoolboy playing hooky from his tutor. Courtiers snickered behind their ruffs, and a sassy epigram whispered through London:

"Elizabeth was King: now James is Queen." In other words, folks joked that the mighty Elizabeth I had shown more manly mettle than her son-like successor James, whom they lampooned as switching roles to *queenly* behavior. (It was a nasty burn by Jacobean standards – one can imagine it trending on Ye Olde Twitter, had social media existed in 1603).

James himself didn't exactly deny his special bond. In a remarkable speech to his Privy Council in 1617, the King attempted a biblical mic-drop to justify his passion for Buckingham: "Jesus Christ did the same... Christ had John, and I have George." Yes, he basically compared his beloved George to Saint John (often called the disciple that Jesus loved) – a bold PR strategy, equating your royal favourite with a holy apostle! James was essentially saying, *"Don't judge me, even JC had a best male friend."* This rationale may have induced some awkward shuffling of feet among the gathered lords – not your everyday defense for spoiling a favorite. But James was king, and he'd found a scriptural spin for his affections.

Behind closed doors, the intimacy was even more blatant. Surviving letters between James and Buckingham read like gushy love notes (albeit in very flowery 17th-century prose). In one letter from 1623, James referred to himself and Buckingham in marital terms, writing, "God bless you, my sweet child and wife, and grant that ye may ever be a comfort to your dear dad and husband." This was the King of England calling his male favorite his *wife* and himself the *husband*! (The dual roles of "dad and husband" might raise an eyebrow – James had a penchant for odd nicknames, calling Buckingham "Steenie," meaning little *Stephen* or angel, because he found him angelically handsome. So, in James's mind, he was *father*, *lover,* and *soulmate* all at once to George – talk about complicated royal family dynamics!) Buckingham reciprocated the affection in kind. In his own letters, he practically swooned on the page: *"I desire only to live in the world for your sake... I will live and die a lover of you,"* he vowed to James. If that isn't a declaration of love, then Romeo and Juliet have nothing on these two.

Of course, not everyone at court was writing sonnets about this relationship. Many viewed Buckingham as a royal favorite-turned-lover who unduly influenced the king. Imagine a modern prime minister appointing his secret paramour to a top cabinet post – eyebrows would shoot up. Similarly, 17th-century Parliamentarians and foreign ambassadors alike grumbled that Buckingham's hold over James was *too* strong. The duo were compared to historical and mythical pairs: Alexander the Great and Hephaestion, or Zeus and his boy-love Ganymede. In fact, one cheeky poem of the era explicitly cast James as the king of the gods besotted with a beautiful youth, warning that the King's infatuation with his "Ganymede" (Buckingham) was causing *political disorder in the court of Olympus*. Another ribald verse (circulated in manuscript, like underground samizdat) cut to the chase by punning that James "f...(ahem) loves the Duke of Buckingham solely for [his] look". It seems Jacobean poets had zero chill – they were basically the stand-up comedians of their day, roasting the royal romance with audacious wordplay.

And yet, despite the whispers, epigrams, and side-eye from pious subjects, James persisted. He loaded Buckingham with honors – gentleman of the bedchamber, viscount, earl, marquess, and finally Duke of Buckingham – a meteoric rise explicitly built, as one historian noted, *"on the handsomeness of his person,"* which utterly captivated the King. James gave Buckingham power over royal patronage, showered him in riches, and even tolerated the Duke's occasional political missteps because, well, love (or intense favoritism) is blind. The arrangement drew so much criticism that ever image-conscious James at times tried to *curb the gossip*. But curbing gossip in a royal court is like trying to stop a wildfire with a thimble of water. Sir Simonds D'Ewes, a Puritan observer, wrote in his diary with barely veiled alarm about *"the sin of sodomy, how frequent it was in this wicked city... especially it being, as we had probable cause to fear, a sin in the prince."* In plainer terms: "We're all gonna be smote by God because King Jimmy can't keep his hands off that Buckingham boy!"

Yet, remarkably, James got away with it—at least during his lifetime. He was the King, after all, and he managed to frame his *hidden love behind the throne* as if it were just a particularly intense friendship sanctified by biblical precedent. It helped that he did fulfill his kingly duties of producing heirs (three children with Queen Anne of Denmark, though their marriage grew cold). Still, behind the curtains, everyone knew where the King's affections lay at night. One could argue James was *semi-out* by the standards of 1620: his same-sex romance was an open secret, only thinly veiled by formal courtiership. He even joked with courtiers about Buckingham, blushing like a schoolgirl when Buckingham's beauty was praised. The whole scenario was ripe for satire – imagine *The Crown* on Netflix doing a flashback season to James I, it would be part political drama, part romantic comedy of manners.

As James's reign drew on, his indulgence in this "bromance" did have consequences. Buckingham's unchecked influence bred resentment and, after James's death, the Duke's high-flying career ended abruptly when he was assassinated (by a disgruntled officer who, legend says, shouted "*God save the King!*" as he stabbed Buckingham – talk about mixed messages). But in James's own time, the King and his *favorite* blazed a trail (or at least a discreet footpath) for queer love in a royal context. They demonstrated that even a king known for Bible-thumping (James commissioned the King James Bible) could harbor a secret that flew in the face of his fire-and-brimstone sermons. The cognitive dissonance is almost comical: James once denounced male sodomy as among the worst sins, *all while cuddling up with Buckingham by the royal bedside.* Hypocrisy, thy name is Majesty!

In the final tally, King James I's hidden love didn't topple his throne, but it did leave a lasting historical wink to later generations. He stands as an early example that even in eras of extreme repression, a powerful person's truth will strain against the closet door. As one modern historian notes, few now doubt James was "either gay or bisexual", and the consensus is that James and Villiers *"were indeed passionate lovers."* Centuries before Pride marches or rainbow flags, a King of England was effectively living a double life – part sovereign ruler, part star-crossed lover – and getting away with it (mostly). It's equal parts inspiring and absurd, and it set the stage for many a royal secret to come.

Before we get too misty-eyed thinking James was a lone warrior for love, let's remember he still had to officially play the role of a straight king married to his queen. His truth stayed *between the lines* of official records, glimpsed only in love letters and quips at court. But hold that thought, because in our next story, we'll meet a royal who didn't even bother with a proper closet. For him, the *open secret* was the only way he knew how to live – until a scandalous splash forced him into exile. Grab your time-machine remote and fast-forward about 250 years…

Archduke Ludwig Viktor – The Habsburg Who Wore a Ball Gown

A 19th-century photograph shows an Austrian archduke resplendent in a frilly ball gown, holding a fan and a bouquet. Such private tableaux vivant captured the side of royal life never seen at stiff state dinners – a prince embracing his inner diva with unapologetic flair.

Welcome to the Austro-Hungarian Empire in the mid-to-late 1800s, where tradition reigned supreme and the imperial family, the Habsburgs, were basically the *CEOs of Conservatism.* Enter Archduke Ludwig Viktor of Austria, the youngest brother of the long-reigning Emperor Franz Joseph. Within the family, Ludwig Viktor was endearingly nicknamed "Luziwuzi" (pronounced *Loot-zi Voot-zi* – possibly the cutest nickname ever bestowed upon a royal). From the start, Luziwuzi marched to the beat of his own drum – or perhaps waltzed to the tune of his own operetta. He was the proverbial "pink sheep" of the imperial flock, an *eccentric oddball* by Habsburg standards, and his homosexuality was an open secret in those gilded halls.

Picture a slight, mischievous archduke who snubbed macho military pursuits and instead reveled in arts, theater, and fabulous parties. Ludwig Viktor had a "face only a mother could love" (one wag quipped this about his less-than-Hollywood looks, and indeed he wasn't movie-star handsome – a bit of a snaggle-toothed Habsburg jaw, by some accounts). Perhaps in compensation, his doting mother, Archduchess Sophie, wanted a girl so badly that she often dressed young Ludwig in girls' outfits. So, if you saw a painting of a pretty little "girl" in a frilly dress at the Habsburg court circa 1845, surprise – that's baby Luziwuzi cross-dressed by Mom. You might say he grew up *extremely comfortable* in his identity; gender-bending theatrics were almost a family tradition for him from the cradle!

As Ludwig Viktor matured, he made little attempt to play the straight-laced soldier-prince. While his elder brothers dutifully married and fulfilled dynastic expectations (or at least tried to), Luziwuzi stayed a bachelor, happily free of any princess bride. Instead, he cultivated a lifestyle that was flamboyantly cultured and only coyly veiled to the public. The archduke loved throwing soirées that were the talk of Vienna's high society. He became a patron of the arts, collected paintings and antiques like they were going out of style, and could deliver a biting bon mot at family dinners with a *sassy wit* that left relatives either chuckling or fuming. One contemporary described him as *"impetuous"* and *"openly homosexual"* with a life that *"revolved around the theatre"*, noting that he even wore women's clothing at times. Indeed, surviving photographs (like the one above) show Ludwig Viktor in full drag – decked in a lace gown, flowers in his hair, looking ready to outshine any Empress at the next masquerade ball. Had RuPaul been around in 1870, this archduke would have *owned* the runway, no doubt.

Within the Habsburg clan, Ludwig Viktor's orientation was tacitly tolerated for quite a while. Emperor Franz Joseph, a rigid stickler in many ways, chose to turn a blind eye out of brotherly love. The family's official stance was *"don't ask, don't tell"* – or rather *don't openly talk about it and the press won't either*, thanks to heavy-handed censorship. Newspapers dared not print the archduke's escapades; at most they'd drop veiled hints about his "unmanly" demeanor. In hushed gossip, though, everyone knew Luziwuzi was gay as a maypole. High-society mothers kept their soldier sons at arm's length from his invitations, for fear the archduke's parties might involve more than polite parlor games. In fact, officers stationed in Salzburg (where Ludwig Viktor had a glorious baroque summer palace) were quietly *forbidden* from attending his lavish soirées, given the archduke's "unnatural inclinations". One can imagine the whispered warnings: *"Don't accept if Luziwuzi invites you for a midnight supper – who knows what you'll find!"*

For a long time, Ludwig Viktor got away with being the lovable, eccentric uncle of the empire, as long as his antics stayed semi-discreet. But then came the scandal that blew the lid off. In 1906, our archduke, by then in his 60s, visited the Centralbad, a popular men-only bathhouse in Vienna (think: 19th-century spa meets gentleman's club, with a bit of steam-room cruising on the side). Ludwig Viktor was a regular there, enjoying "Turkish baths" and likely the *eye candy* of strapping young bathers. On this day, however, he crossed a line – he made a flirtatious advance on a young man of respectable middle-class background. The advance was *not* appreciated. In fact, the offended gentleman responded by slapping the Archduke squarely in the face, knocking him to the floor of the bathhouse in a tussle. Yes, a commoner literally *boxed the ears* of the Emperor's baby brother in public, sending imperial dignity flying out the window along with, presumably, the archduke's towel.

This was Defcon-1 level scandal. A Habsburg getting decked by some random guy in a public bathhouse brawl? The rumor mills exploded. Ludwig Viktor, humiliated and furious, pulled rank and had the fellow arrested – but that backfired spectacularly. Authorities quietly released the man, deciding his reaction was *warranted* under the circumstances. Word of the brawl – *in the most lurid colors*, as you can imagine – reached Emperor Franz Joseph. The 76-year-old emperor, who had stoically endured all of Luziwuzi's previous capers, finally hit the roof. Enough was enough: to avoid further embarrassment to the Crown, Franz Joseph banished Ludwig Viktor from Vienna immediately, exiling him to the remote Schloss Klessheim in Salzburg. The Emperor even snarked that his wayward brother should be given a *ballerina* as an aide-de-camp to keep him out of trouble (the imperial equivalent of "give the man a tutu and maybe he'll behave!").

And so, the archduke spent his twilight years in lonely splendor, far from the intrigues of the capital. He lived out his days at Schloss Klessheim under a kind of house arrest (albeit a gilded one, with extensive gardens). In 1915, during World War I, the family quietly declared him insane – perhaps to further invalidate any statements he might make or simply to formalize his removal from public life. Ludwig Viktor died in 1919, just after the Habsburg monarchy collapsed, almost as if he lingered long enough to see the old order that shunned him finally crumble. One can't help seeing a bit of poetic justice: the empire that punished him for being true to himself didn't endure, but Luziwuzi's story lives on as a vivid reminder of the absurd lengths royals once went to in order to keep up appearances.

It's worth noting that despite the scandal, Ludwig Viktor never really *repented* who he was. In his younger days he had flatly refused marriages arranged for him – including one to Duchess Sophie of Bavaria (Empress Sisi's sister), which he dodged, likely with a sigh of relief. (In a twist of fate, that same Duchess Sophie later got engaged to King Ludwig II of Bavaria – another gay royal – who also jilted her. Poor Sophie, she couldn't catch a hetero break!). Ludwig Viktor instead surrounded himself with friends and lovers in his private life. He had a known long-term romance with a handsome nobleman, Count Eduard von Paar, which was *"warmly acknowledged by close circles"* if not the public. In other words, within his trusted coterie, Ludwig Viktor did find love and acceptance, even if the wider society forced it into the shadows.

The archduke's saga is equal parts tragic and campy. On one hand, it reads like a farce: a prince in petticoats causing a scandalous bar fight – you couldn't script a better black-and-white silent film comedy. On the other, there's an undertone of sadness: a talented, vivacious man consigned to solitude because his truth embarrassed an empire. If King James's story was about quietly subverting norms from the top, Ludwig Viktor's tale is about the limits of imperial tolerance and how a flamboyant royal *pushed those limits until they snapped.* He showed that even a prince, for all his privilege, could be harshly punished for straying from society's straight and narrow.

As we chuckle at the image of an aristocrat in a tutu outrunning scandal, we also nod to his courage (or perhaps stubbornness) in *never denying who he was*. Ludwig Viktor's hidden love wasn't even that hidden – it was a scandal only when the larger public caught a glimpse. His life reminds us that repression in royal life often led to double lives and secrecy... but also that some truths were just too vibrant to stay totally contained. The slow march toward openness hit a roadblock in his era – resulting in a painful exile – yet the whispers never erased the man's identity. In a way, Ludwig Viktor set the stage for the future by embodying the idea that a royal could be unapologetically different, even if the world wasn't ready to accept it.

Now, speaking of the world becoming ready – it's time to leap into the modern age, where thankfully no one gets exiled to a countryside palace for falling in love. Our final story brings us to the 21st century, with a member of the British royal family who didn't have to hide or fight – instead, he got to celebrate his truth with confetti and a wedding cake (made of cheese, no less!).

Lord Ivar Mountbatten – Breaking the Royal Closet (Love Wins at Last)

History can sometimes move at a glacial pace, but when it *does* reach a milestone, it's worth a cheer. In 2018, the extended British royal family quietly (and somewhat surprisingly) celebrated its first same-sex wedding – proof that even the most tradition-bound institution can inch toward progress. The trailblazer was Lord Ivar Mountbatten, a cousin of Queen Elizabeth II. If King James had to slip love notes under the table and Archduke Luziwuzi got slapped into exile, Lord Ivar's journey shows us how far society (and royalty) have come: he came out publicly, found love, and tied the knot with another man *with his family's blessing*. It was the ultimate feel-good finale for our trio of tales – like the happy ending we've been waiting for, complete with a modern royal twist.

Who is Lord Ivar Mountbatten? He's not a household name like Prince William or Harry, but he is royalty-adjacent – the great-nephew of Lord Louis Mountbatten (famed 1st Earl Mountbatten of Burma) and a *third cousin once removed* to the Queen. In plain terms, a bit of a *B-list royal*, the kind who shows up in family trees and occasionally in the society pages. For years, Ivar led a pretty typical aristocratic life: he married a woman (Penny Thompson) in the 1990s, had three lovely daughters, and kept up public duties like charity events and even a stint on a reality TV show. But inside, he was carrying a truth he hadn't yet voiced publicly. In 2016, six years after divorcing Penny, Lord Ivar came out as bisexual (he's often called gay in media, but he has clarified he is bi). The news made a few headlines – "Queen's Cousin Comes Out" – but in a sign of changing times, it was met largely with positivity or a collective shrug. No exile, no scandal forcing the monarch to make awkward speeches; if anything, the British public seemed rather pleased to see a royal living authentically. The slow march toward openness had finally reached Buckingham Palace's extended family.

Not long after coming out, Ivar found love with James Coyle, a Scottish airline cabin services director he met on a vacation in 2014. By 2018, the two decided to take a step that would have been unthinkable for James I or Ludwig Viktor: they planned a full-fledged wedding. Yes, a royal same-sex wedding, complete with a country estate venue, elegant suits (velvet smoking jackets in green and navy, to be exact), and a beaming family in attendance. If you need a mental image, picture a quaint chapel on Lord Ivar's own estate in Devon, a gospel choir singing (they actually had one, rocking the house), and two grooms walking down the aisle under a slight drizzle of English rain, sharing an umbrella and big smiles. In September 2018, this vision became reality: Lord Ivar married James Coyle in front of about 60 family members and friends. In doing so, he earned the distinction of being the first member of the British royal family to have a same-sex marriage.

The event was groundbreaking but refreshingly low-key. No televised spectacle, no Westminster Abbey fanfare – just an intimate gathering. Yet it had its share of *royal flair*. In a delightful twist, Lord Ivar's ex-wife, Penny, walked him down the aisle and "gave him away" to James. This was actually Penny and their daughters' idea; the girls wanted their mom to have that honor since their dad had done it for them years before. So, there was Penny, in a lovely dress, escorting her former husband to marry his new husband – talk about modern family values! Lord Ivar later expressed how *touched* he was by this gesture, and honestly, if that doesn't melt your heart, check your pulse. The image of an ex-wife handing off her ex-husband to his male spouse with everyone smiling – it's like something out of a progressive fairy tale. Even Disney hasn't done that (yet).

The wedding got a flurry of positive press. One reason it wasn't a scandal at all is because the royals had slowly been laying groundwork for tolerance. The Queen herself had publicly signaled support for LGBTQ equality (in a Queenly, indirect way) by mentioning in a 2017 speech that her government would tackle "discrimination... on the basis of sexual orientation". Princes William and Harry have spoken up in support of LGBTQ people. So, by 2018, the House of Windsor was *at least officially* on the right side of history. And here came Lord Ivar, turning that talk into action in his personal life. There was no pushback from the family – in fact, some senior royals like Prince Edward and his wife Sophie (close cousins to Ivar) were privately very supportive, though they couldn't attend due to scheduling.

On social media – yes, our modern monarchists live on Instagram – Lord Ivar shared joyful photos of the day, complete with humorous captions. "Well, we did it finally!" he wrote, celebrating the long-awaited union. He joked about the *"miserable British weather"* (it rained, naturally) but said it was an *amazing day* nonetheless. He heaped thanks on the choir, the officiant, and especially his three "gorgeous girls" (daughters) for being so supportive, noting "without their support this could never have happened!". Then, in a line that feels like a closing chapter to centuries of secret loves, he gave "the biggest thank you to James for being just perfect". Alongside were photos of Ivar and James in their sharp jackets, holding hands under an umbrella, grinning ear to ear, as happy as any newlyweds could be. Even the family dog wore a rainbow ribbon for the occasion, tuckered out after enthusiastically participating in the ceremony (and vacuuming up cake crumbs). It was wholesome, heartwarming, and historic all at once.

For a royal family that had *plenty* of gay members in its distant past who had to hide or suffer, this moment was almost healing. Here was a Mountbatten – descended from Queen Victoria like so many European royals – openly declaring his truth and being *celebrated* for it. No code words, no "shameful exile to the continent" as might have happened a hundred years prior. Times had changed enough that the reaction from the public was basically, "Good on them, congrats!" in the papers and a shrug from the palace (which in Royal-speak is tacit approval). Lord Ivar himself reflected that he pushed for the wedding more for James's sake than his own, since James had never been married and "I want to be able to give you that," he told him. It was a gesture of love and commitment, pure and simple – the gender of the couple finally a non-issue, at least to those who mattered.

This story brings our narrative full circle. Where King James I had to couch his love in biblical metaphors and secret letters, and Archduke Ludwig Viktor got physically slapped and banished for his desires, Lord Ivar could openly kiss his husband in front of family and say "I do" without fear. It's almost dizzying to consider the contrast. The royal closet door, thick and reinforced by centuries of tradition, finally swung open – if not for a reigning monarch (we're not *quite* there yet), at least for a member of the royal family who felt safe stepping out into the spotlight. And once truth came out, it wasn't the downfall of the monarchy or any such nonsense; it was, in fact, met with affection and a rousing gospel choir.

Lord Ivar's openness also subtly pressures the broader institution: it says *look, this is possible.* A royal (even if a minor one) can be true to themselves and the sky doesn't fall. In interviews, he mentioned how much happier he was after coming out, and how supportive his ex-wife and kids were – a modern family navigating change with love. It sends a hopeful message downstream: future royals grappling with identity might not need to hide at all. One day, perhaps even a high-ranking royal could come out and marry whom they love, and it would be just another joyous occasion. The slow march toward openness may have been glacial, but it reached a sunny destination on that September day in Devon.

As we bask in the warm fuzzies of this modern love story, it's time to reflect on the journey we've taken – from secret passions whispered in code to Instagram-official weddings. What does it all mean? Let's conclude our chapter with the moral of these tales as we tie the threads together, with a neat bow (rainbow-colored, naturally).

From the Shadows to the Spotlight – The Enduring Light of Truth

Looking back over these royal romances, one can't help but appreciate the dramatic change across eras. In King James's time, the truth had to wear a mask and speak in poetic whispers; in Archduke Ludwig Viktor's, it burst out flamboyantly but was shoved back into a box by scandal; and in Lord Ivar Mountbatten's, it finally walked free, hand-in-hand with a loved one, in daylight. Each story illuminates a broader truth about identity and social norms. Royalty, often seen as the epitome of tradition, turned out to have the same diversity of heart as the rest of humanity. The difference was, for the longest time they had to hide it under crowns and ermine. But no secret stays buried forever – especially not one as integral as whom you love.

These tales carry a clear moral: honesty is more enduring than tradition. Traditions can suppress, deny, or punish, but eventually, the human spirit finds a way to shine through. King James's letters survived centuries to tell us what official chronicles would not. Ludwig Viktor's nickname and escapades leaked into legend, so even imperial censorship couldn't erase his fabulous footprint (he's arguably more famous today for being himself than any of his straight-laced brothers are for toeing the line). And Lord Ivar's open wedding became a milestone that the history books will note as a turning point for royal acceptance. Truth, however hidden, *longs for light*. It's as if these secret loves were seeds planted in the dark soil of history, waiting for the right conditions to sprout. And sprout they did – first a pale shoot here, a crack in the facade there, and finally a full bloom in the modern sun.

There is also a delightful irony that the very institution designed to project an image of perfect, traditional family values had so many colorful variations behind the scenes. It reminds us that royals are human – bound by duty but driven by the same need for love and authenticity as anyone else. Their elevated status made the clash between truth and tradition more visible, more poignant, and sometimes more absurd (sixteenth-century poems calling a king a sodomite, nineteenth-century generals gossiping about an archduke's cross-dressing, etc.). In those contrasts, we see society's changing tides. What was a scandal becomes a shrug over time. The slow march toward openness in royal life mirrors that in society at large: progress inches along, then suddenly, *finally*, a door opens.

As a single narrative, these three stories flow into one another like acts of a long play about secrecy and revelation. Act I (James and Buckingham) shows a world where a king's love is *technically* hidden but peeks through in winks and coded lines. Act II (Ludwig Viktor) is a mixture of comedy and drama, where the truth is barely hidden at all until it explodes in public view, resulting in a tragicomic downfall. Act III (Lord Ivar) is the triumphant finale – the secret is no longer secret, the love is celebrated openly, and nobody loses their head (or their title) over it. The *arc of history* here bends toward openness, validating the idea that authenticity will have its day.

In a conversational, modern sense: if we could invite King James, Archduke Luziwuzi, and Lord Ivar for tea, one imagines James would blush at how open Ivar can be, Ludwig Viktor would applaud wildly and immediately volunteer to plan Ivar's anniversary party (costumes included), and Ivar, the gracious host, might simply smile and say, "Well, it took a few centuries, but welcome to the light, Your Majesties." It's a fanciful image, but it underscores the point – each successive story builds on the bravery (and yes, follies) of the previous. The struggles of those who had to hide made it easier for those who followed to be seen.

In the end, *Same-Sex Secrets – Hidden Loves Behind the Throne* isn't just about juicy gossip in palaces (though we had plenty of that with a wink and a nudge). It's about the enduring truth that love and identity, even when forced into secrecy, will persist. Kings and princes can't fully suppress who they are any more than anyone else can – and when they ultimately embrace honesty, they often find it wasn't the end of the world, but the beginning of a happier one. The moral shines clearly: Tradition may be mighty, but truth is mightier. However slowly it travels, however long it hides in corridors and boudoirs, the truth wants to be free – and when it is, it lights up the halls more brilliantly than any gilded chandelier. So, here's to the hidden loves behind thrones, now coming into the open: proof that even in royal life, *love wins* in the end.

- Accounts of King James I's relationship with George Villiers, Duke of Buckingham, including contemporary epigrams and letters, indicate that their bond went beyond politics into passionate love. Historians now widely agree James had romantic/sexual relationships with his male favorites. James's public displays of affection and the power he granted Buckingham drew both admiration and satire in his time.

- Archduke Ludwig Viktor of Austria ("Luziwuzi"), youngest brother of Emperor Franz Joseph, was openly gay within his family circle – a fact shrouded by 19th-century press censorship. He defied conservative norms by cross-dressing and hosting all-male festivities. The infamous 1906 bathhouse scandal – where Ludwig Viktor was slapped after making an advance – led to his banishment from Vienna by the Emperor. His story illustrates the Habsburgs' reluctant tolerance giving way to repression when private conduct became a public embarrassment.

- Lord Ivar Mountbatten, a cousin of Queen Elizabeth II, made history with the first same-sex wedding in the British royal family. In 2018, he married his partner James Coyle in a private ceremony in Devon, with his ex-wife Penny walking him down the aisle. Lord Ivar had come out in 2016, and his wedding – attended by family and affirmed on his Instagram – marked a milestone of modern royal acceptance. The positive reception of this event highlights the evolving social norms and increased openness toward LGBTQ identities in royal circles.

Chapter 10

Manipulation and Intrigue – When Love is a Weapon

Love and war have always shared a flair for drama, but history gets especially juicy when *love itself* becomes a weapon of war. In this chapter, we'll visit three very different courts — imperial China, the Ottoman harem, and Renaissance France — to meet women who turned romance into a battlefield and seduction into statecraft. Don't expect fairy-tale love stories here; these are tales of power games, survival, and seduction with a satirical twist. Grab some popcorn (or perhaps a cup of poisoned wine) and prepare for a romp through history where Cupid wears armor and affairs of the heart double as affairs of state.

We'll start with Wu Zetian in imperial China, who rose from concubine to emperor (yes, emperor) by outmaneuvering lovers and rivals at every turn. Then we'll step into the sumptuous (and perilous) world of the Ottoman harem, a royal reality show where wives and concubines schemed like contestants on *The Bachelor* — except the prize was supreme power (and you really didn't want to be voted off this island). Finally, we'll meet Catherine de' Medici in France, the so-called "Black Queen" who practically made marriage treaties and femme-fatale espionage into an Olympic sport. Through humorous commentary and contemporary analogies, we'll see how these women navigated patriarchal systems with clever subterfuge and strategic flair. By the end, the shared moral should shine through: when love becomes commodified, it turns into a dangerous tool of ambition — and heaven help anyone in its path.

Wu Zetian: The Concubine Who Became King

Wu Zetian was *not* your standard-issue demure concubine. Think of her as the ultimate palace underdog who flipped the script on a patriarchal empire. In 7th-century China's Tang Dynasty, a concubine was expected to serve quietly and, when the emperor died, retreat to a nunnery to live out her days praying — basically ancient China's version of being sent to a farm upstate. Wu Zetian had other plans. When Emperor Taizong died, she boldly defied tradition by sidestepping the nunnery and catching the eye of the next emperor (who, conveniently, was Taizong's son, Gaozong). Rumor has it Wu and the young Gaozong had already been *more than friends* before old Dad kicked the bucket. Scandalous? Oh, absolutely — and a sign of things to come.

Once back in the palace, Wu Zetian set out to win the game of courtly romance with a singular focus. The new Emperor Gaozong already had a wife, Empress Wang, and a favored concubine, Lady Xiao, who together were the Regina George of this imperial *Mean Girls* clique. Empress Wang initially thought bringing Wu back from the convent would be a smart move — you know, to distract the emperor from *other* women. Oops. Wu not only distracted him; she became his obsession. With the emperor wrapped around her finger, Wu's next step was to eliminate the competition (palace life is *survival of the fittest,* and in this case the fittest was a 20-something woman with a master plan). What came next is the stuff of legend and *morbid gossip*: Wu gave birth to a baby girl who died mysteriously soon after. Instead of a grieving mother, palace insiders got a criminal mastermind — Wu deftly accused Empress Wang of murdering the child, a charge which, true or not, achieved its desired effect. Gaozong, horrified and heartbroken, booted his wife off the throne and banished both Wang and Lady Xiao to a lonely prison cell. Wu Zetian, mission accomplished, stepped into the vacancy as the new Empress. (Historians now largely suspect Wu herself strangled her infant to frame the Empress, a move so cold-blooded it makes Cersei Lannister look like Mother of the Year.)

Becoming Empress was only Level One of Wu's game. Once in power, she had zero intention of sharing the spotlight. Empress Wang and Lady Xiao were still alive in prison — a situation Wu "remedied" with a brutality that would traumatize *Mortal Kombat* fans. According to later chroniclers (who were definitely not in Wu's fan club), the newly minted Empress had the two rival women's hands and feet cut off and tossed them into vats of wine. (Talk about a *punch bowl* — imperial court edition.) Whether this grisly tale is 100% true or a smear campaign by Wu's enemies, it cemented her reputation as someone who didn't mess around when it came to consolidating power. As she supposedly quipped (in the movie version in my head), *"It's nothing personal, ladies — it's just politics."* The court got the message: love was Wu's weapon, and she wielded it with ruthless efficiency.

With rivals out of the way, Wu Zetian and Emperor Gaozong ruled together — though before long it was clear who wore the imperial pants. When Gaozong's health declined, Wu became the power behind the throne, then *on* the throne. She declared herself Emperor of China (not Empress Consort, mind you, but Emperor in her own right) in 690, founding her own Zhou Dynasty. This was utterly unprecedented — a female ruler of the Middle Kingdom was about as unthinkable as a dragon flying over the Forbidden City. Confucian scholars practically fainted en masse; one described a woman on the throne as "an aberration of natural and human order". Wu's response? Essentially, *cry harder*. She made sure everyone knew who was boss, even introducing new characters into the Chinese writing system with her name embedded, just to leave a permanent mark on history.

Of course, being a pioneering woman in power meant historians of her time (mostly dudes) painted Wu Zetian as a treacherous seductress, a murderer, and worse. To be fair, she *did* probably murder and torture a number of people (hazard of the job when you seize power in medieval China). But one has to wonder how much of her *dragon lady* reputation was exaggerated by the patriarchy — jealous ministers clutching their pearls that a woman outsmarted them all. Case in point: when Wu died at the ripe age of 80, her successors left her memorial tablet blank. No inscription of achievements, nothing – basically the imperial equivalent of an unfriending. Thousands of years later, though, Wu Zetian is remembered not just for her (many) alleged crimes but for shattering the ultimate glass ceiling of her era.

Before we bid farewell to Wu, we have to talk about her *late-life power moves*, which put a wicked twist on the whole saga. In her seventies (an age when most emperors were long dead or retired), Wu took on a pair of boy-toy lovers in their twenties, known as the Zhang brothers. Yes, you read that right – grandma got her groove back, Tang Dynasty-style. Picture the aging Empress, possibly bored after decades of ruling, deciding, "You know what? I deserve some fun." She brought these two handsome young men into her boudoir and, according to scandalized reports, spent her final years *indulging* while they took care of her...administrative needs. Courtiers whispered that the once-formidable ruler was neglecting state affairs for pleasure palace antics. It was a reversal of roles so complete, it's almost poetic: the woman who climbed to power as a concubine ended her reign by turning the tables and *keeping her own concubines*. One might call it Empress Wu's Retirement Plan — less Bingo and gardening, more champagne and late-night parties in the imperial chambers. Ultimately, this *octogenarian spree* gave her displaced son the opening to stage a coup. Wu Zetian was forced to abdicate in 705, closing the chapter on a reign that was equal parts revolutionary and appalling.

Wu Zetian's story has everything: humble origins, seduction, betrayal, family drama, political intrigue, and a healthy dose of violence (plus a final act that feels like a raunchy sitcom spinoff). It's no wonder her tale has inspired countless novels, dramas, and debates. Through a modern lens, we can chuckle at the absurdity of some legends (murdering your baby to frame the boss – really?!), but we also recognize a serious core: Wu was a woman who weaponized love and sexuality to climb a ladder rigged against her, and she did it so effectively that she became emperor of one of the world's greatest empires. She played the game of love like chess, turning romantic favor into checkmate against all her foes. The men of her time never saw it coming – and likely never got over it. As we leave Wu's lavish and lethal court, keep in mind her signature lesson: in a world that expected women to be pawns, she became the chess master.

From the palaces of Chang'an to the confines of Topkapi…

If you thought one woman turning an entire imperial hierarchy on its head was wild, wait until you see a whole team of women doing much the same. Buckle up for a journey to the Ottoman Empire, where the sultan's harem was less "seraglio of delights" and more "Survivor: Istanbul" – complete with alliances, backstabbing, and the occasional silken bowstring elimination ceremony.

The Ottoman Harem: Love, Lies, and *Lockdown* in the Sultan's Palace

Welcome to the Topkapi Palace in the 16th century, the seat of the Ottoman sultans and home to the Imperial Harem – a world as opulent as a jewelry box and as treacherous as a viper's nest. If you're imagining a lazy paradise of lounging ladies eating Turkish delight all day, think again. The harem was a high-stakes political arena where romantic favor meant influence, and influence meant *everything*. Dozens (sometimes hundreds) of women – wives, concubines, the sultan's mother, sisters, and daughters – lived in this gilded cage. Outwardly, they were secluded, veiled, and submissive according to the era's norms. Behind closed doors, these women were playing power politics with the subtlety of a Machiavellian chess club. It was like a season of *Real Housewives*, except the "house" was an empire and every contestant desperately wanted to birth the next Sultan (preferably while ensuring the current one loved her best and maybe arranging an *unfortunate accident* for any rivals). Romance was currency, sex was leverage, and the harem's motto might as well have been *"In love and war, all is permitted – as long as the eunuchs don't find out."*

This era became so dominated by powerful women that historians literally call it the Sultanate of Women. For about a century (roughly 1530s to 1650s), the Ottoman Empire sometimes seemed *less* like a one-man show and *more* like a family corporation run by its fiercest female CEOs. Here's the usual script: A girl (often a slave from somewhere like Russia, Ukraine, or the Caucasus) is brought into the harem as a teenager. She's taught the fine arts of court etiquette, music, dance, and how to not stab the sultan with a hairpin when he says something stupid. If she's lucky or especially charming, she catches the ruler's eye. Maybe she spends a night (or a few) with him. Maybe she gets pregnant — jackpot! Because under the peculiar Ottoman system, a concubine who bore a son gained tremendous status. In fact, each mother was only supposed to have one son; mother and child would traditionally be sent off to the provinces, where the prince would grow up (and the mother could no longer scheme at court). This was meant to prevent any one woman from gaining too much influence, and to keep the sons from murdering each other too early. But what happens if a sultan breaks the rules and actually *falls in love*?

Enter Hürrem Sultan, better known to the West as Roxelana, the OG of Ottoman harem power players. Roxelana's story plays out like a cross between *Cinderella* and *House of Cards*. She began as a slave girl from the Ukraine (possibly kidnapped by Crimean Tatars) and ended up the beloved wife of Sultan Suleiman the Magnificent – yeah, the guy literally called "the Magnificent." Suleiman was no slouch himself, ruling from 1520 to 1566 and expanding the empire to its zenith, but apparently even *he* wasn't immune to some quality time and a good conversation after work. Roxelana captivated him, and he did something unheard of: he stopped sleeping with his other concubines altogether. This was *beyond* shocking. Previous sultans kept harems for pleasure and heirs, not for true monogamy. Suleiman, lovestruck, essentially said "One is enough" and even married Roxelana in a legal ceremony (again, totally breaking with tradition – sultans didn't officially marry their concubines before her). You might say Roxelana "*Hurrem*-ed" his affection to the point that he threw out the old playbook. The other women of the harem were, unsurprisingly, fuming at this development. Imagine a reality show where the bachelor suddenly cancels the show halfway through because he's found The One, and the remaining contestants are told to pack their bags — but first, he marries the winner on live TV. That's the vibe.

Roxelana's rise was meteoric. In short order she bore Suleiman multiple children — a whopping six in total, five of them sons. This was practically a scandal in itself; she shattered the "one mother, one son" rule into tiny pieces. More sons meant more potential heirs, which historically meant fratricidal *Game of Thrones* showdowns after the throne change. But Roxelana wasn't just multiplying the potential for civil war; she was also consolidating *her own* power. She knew that if one of her boys became the next sultan, she'd ascend to the coveted role of Valide Sultan (Queen Mother), effectively the most powerful woman in the empire. The only fly in the ointment was Mustafa – the eldest son of Suleiman from an earlier liaison (with a concubine named Mahidevran).

Prince Mustafa was popular, competent, and first in line, which made him a mortal threat to Roxelana's ambitions (and to her sons' necks, quite literally). What did Roxelana do? Let's just say she didn't leave it to chance. Leveraging Suleiman's trust and perhaps feeding on his paranoia, Roxelana (with the help of her ally/son-in-law, the Grand Vizier Rüstem Pasha) cooked up a treacherous plot. They allegedly forged letters to make it appear that Prince Mustafa was in cahoots with the Persian Shah, plotting to usurp his father. In essence, she weaponized Suleiman's fatherly love and turned it into fear. In 1553, during a military campaign, Suleiman summoned Mustafa to his tent and — in a scene no doubt devoid of Hallmark moments — ordered his execution. The prince was strangled with a silk bowstring, as was the custom (Ottoman noble blood was not to be spilled on the ground; if you have to kill your kid, at least do it elegantly). Roxelana's chief rival was thus eliminated, and her own sons' path to the throne was clear. It was a brutal play, arguably the most infamous harem intrigue of the Ottoman era. Imagine a mother convincing her husband to kill his firstborn son based on likely forged evidence — that's some next-level dysfunctional family drama. Even *Shakespeare* might have found it a tad over-the-top.

With Mustafa gone, Roxelana's influence only grew. Suleiman not only adored her; he *trusted* her counsel on state matters. Foreign ambassadors knew that to get to the Sultan, you might want to slip a note to Hürrem first. She engaged in charitable works, built mosques, and even corresponded with the Polish king in her own name (unheard of for a sultana). Roxelana died before Suleiman (she never got to be Valide Sultan for her son, unfortunately), but she blazed a trail. After her came a succession of formidable harem matriarchs:

Nurbanu Sultan (who ruled through her son Murad III), Kösem Sultan (an absolute tour de force who was regent for her son and grandson and basically ran the empire for decades until she got strangled by a rival in the harem — yes, *another* bowstring!), and others. These women carried on the tradition that Roxelana had solidified: using romantic and maternal influence to control the empire from behind the lattice screen. The harem became, in effect, the women's quarter of the government. Foreigners at the time were alternately fascinated and horrified. One French ambassador in the 1600s probably spit out his wine when he realized he had to negotiate not just with the Sultan, but also with his mom.

To put it in a modern analogy, the Ottoman harem during the Sultanate of Women was like a super elite boarding school combined with a corporate boardroom, except the CEO is a Sultan who might hand out roses one night and death sentences the next. The competition among the women could be deadly, but it could also forge surprising alliances (sometimes the sultan's mother and his favorite consort worked together to run the show; sometimes they were mortal enemies – depends on the TV season). Eunuchs, the only men allowed in the harem, acted as the go-betweens and were often the women's trusted agents (or co-conspirators). Picture a reality show where the host is also secretly helping certain contestants scheme — that's the Chief Black Eunuch for you.

Life in the harem was luxurious captivity. These women were educated, dressed in the finest silks, and literally lived among jewels and perfumes, but they were also essentially prisoners of the palace, barred from the outside world. Thus, their world turned inward, into palace intrigue. Love and affection in this context became

175

transactional. A concubine might genuinely fall for the sultan (Suleiman and Roxelana do sound like they had a real romance amid the intrigue), but she also knew that her entire fate hung on his favor. Likewise, the sultan might love his consort, but that didn't stop him from executing their son if he believed the kid posed a threat (Ottoman politics were hardcore like that — they had a notorious practice of fratricide where new sultans would execute all their brothers to secure the throne; family reunions were *tense* to say the least).

In the Ottoman harem, romantic relationships were wielded as tools of influence, status, and control every single day. The women who thrived did so by outmaneuvering others with wit and charm, much as Wu Zetian did, but in a far more collective and constrained environment. They couldn't raise armies, but they could raise sons — and shape future sultans to be loyal to *them*. They couldn't make speeches in the divan (council), but they could whisper into the right ear at night. Seduction and motherhood were their weapons, and they were fiercely effective.

By the time the Sultanate of Women era ended (the system changed in the mid-17th century; sultans stopped having multiple concubine mothers for heirs and moved to a seniority system for succession — less bloody, but also reducing harem infighting), the Ottoman Empire had been indelibly shaped by these women's machinations. Some sultans literally owed their throne to their mother's deadly scheming. Diplomats knew a Valide Sultan (queen mother) could make or break treaties. The harem, supposedly a private realm, was in fact a political nerve center.

Our featured story in this realm — Roxelana and the harem politics around Suleiman — highlights the moral in a satirical light. Here's a woman who started as human booty from a raid (not exactly a position of power), who used love and devotion as a ladder to become the most powerful woman in the empire. And she wasn't content to just *be* powerful herself; she wanted her progeny to rule, and she bent the empire to that purpose. It's hard not to admire the audacity, even as you cringe at the human cost (poor Mustafa might have a thing or two to say about "ambition"). It's equally hard not to see parallels with, say, modern corporate politics or celebrity worlds. (Is it any wonder a popular Turkish TV series, *Magnificent Century*, dramatizing Roxelana's life, became an international hit? It's like *Downton Abbey* meets *Game of Thrones* with extra silk and sherbet.)

So, what comedic takeaway do we have from the harem? Perhaps it's this If you ever feel life is like a competition for attention, remember the ladies of Topkapi. They turned *"He loves me, he loves me not"* into a strategic calculus that could decide the fate of an empire. The stakes in your office romance or PTA flirtation are (hopefully) a tad lower. And should you find a rival blocking your path to glory, you can chuckle and think, *"At least I'm not having her strangled — I'm positively saintly compared to those gals."*

From Istanbul, we now move to Paris...

Having seen love weaponized in an imperial harem, it's time to visit Renaissance France, where one remarkable woman managed to play Cupid, Coach, and Shadow Queen all at once. If the Ottoman harem was a team sport, Catherine de' Medici was a one-woman show (with an ensemble cast of offspring and ladies-in-waiting, of course). She didn't have a hundred concubines to maneuver, but she had something up her ruffled Renaissance sleeve that was just as effective: clever marriages and a "flying squadron" of lovely spies. Oui, mes amis, things are about to get très intéressant.

Catherine de' Medici: Matchmaking, Machinations, and a Dash of Poison

When Catherine de' Medici arrived in France in 1533 as a 14-year-old bride, nobody could have predicted she'd become the queen mother of intrigue. She was an Italian merchant princess (the Medici weren't blue-blood royals, they were rich bankers — basically nouveau riche in the snobby eyes of French nobility). The French court initially treated young Catherine like a nobody: a *"common"* girl lucky to marry Prince Henry (second in line to the throne at the time). To make matters worse, her new husband Henry had a well-known lifelong mistress, Diane de Poitiers, who was two decades older than Catherine and infinitely more experienced in wielding influence. Think of Catherine in those early years as a sort of *Princess Diana... if Prince Charles's mistress had been living at Buckingham the whole time.* Awkward. While Henry II (he became king in 1547) doted on Diane, Catherine was basically a royal broodmare expected to produce heirs and otherwise stay out of the way. It took her *ten years* to conceive an heir – years filled with humiliation, as Diane de Poitiers took center stage in Henry's affection and even political counsel. (Fun fact: Catherine had to swallow all manner of weird fertility potions, including one *very* dubious concoction involving cow dung and ground stag antlers. The girl earned her stripes.) All the while, Catherine watched and learned. She saw how Diane wrapped the king around her little finger — how this older woman could coax favors, appointments, and influence out of a besotted Henry. It clicked for Catherine that sex and love could move mountains at court, even when you technically had no official power.

Then 1559 rolled around, and life did that thing where it flips the table. King Henry II died in a freak jousting accident (it's all fun and games until someone's eye gets put out – literally, in his case). Suddenly, Catherine was no longer the sidelined wife; she was the Queen Mother of a fragile dynasty. Her teenage son Francis II became king (he was married to Mary, Queen of Scots – more drama), but he was sickly. He died after barely a year, and next up was her 10-year-old son Charles IX. Obviously, a 10-year-old can't rule France alone (he'd sign all his edicts in crayon). Traditionally, a close male relative would become regent. But Catherine said, *"Non, merci, I've got this."*

She maneuvered herself into the regency, and thanks to a mix of charm and maybe a strategic seduction or two, even the would-be male regent, Antoine of Navarre, stepped aside for her. (One rumor claims Catherine *dispatched one of her beautiful ladies-in-waiting to seduce Antoine* into giving up his claim. True or not, it's exactly the sort of move that became her signature style — why argue when you can distract?) Catherine was now the de facto ruler of France, calling the shots for her young sons Charles IX and later Henry III. But reigning over France in the late 16th century was like juggling flaming chainsaws; the country was torn apart by religious wars between Catholics and Protestants (Huguenots), nobles were plotting constantly, and Catherine's hold on power was tenuous at best. What's a queen mother to do? Wield love like a weapon, of course — deploying daughters, daughters-in-law, and dainty assassins as needed.

Catherine's first strategy: marry her children into alliances that would strengthen her family's grip. She had *ten* kids (busy times after that slow start!), of whom seven survived to marriageable age. She treated weddings like high-stakes diplomatic summits. As one historian put it, *"weddings were the oldest form of political strategy"* and Catherine understood this in her bones. She successfully placed her daughter Elisabeth as wife to King Philip II of Spain (one of the most powerful monarchs in the world). Another daughter, Claude, married into the powerhouse Guise-related family, the Dukes of Lorraine. She tried *really hard* to snag England's Queen Elizabeth I as a daughter-in-law by offering her son Henry, Duke of Anjou (later Henry III of France), in marriage – multiple times, in fact. Elizabeth I ultimately said, *"I'm flattered, but I'll pass"* (perhaps wisely suspecting that being Catherine's in-law might come with hazard pay). Nonetheless, Catherine's batting average in the marriage game was impressive. She was effectively building a web of in-laws across Europe, hoping to secure France's flank and her Valois dynasty's future through these romantic (or not-so-romantic) unions. It was like a giant chessboard where the queens (literally) were moving the pieces – and Catherine was determined to checkmate her enemies with bridal veils and baby carriages.

However, Catherine's most infamous marital gambit was the 1572 wedding of her daughter Marguerite de Valois (Queen Margot) to Henry of Navarre (head of the Protestant Huguenots, who would later become King Henry IV). This was supposed to be the ultimate peace treaty between France's warring religious factions – a royal marriage to unite Catholics and Protestants in amity. *C'est romantique*, non? Eh, not so much. Margot wasn't thrilled (she had lovers of her own and described her new husband as smelling like a goat – ouch). Henry of Navarre was pragmatic, willing to marry into the French royal family for the sake of peace. Catherine orchestrated the whole thing with grand pomp, inviting all the prominent Huguenots to Paris for the celebrations. For a brief moment, it looked like love (or at least mutual tolerance) might conquer hate.

Then came what we now call the St. Bartholomew's Day Massacre. Mere days after the wedding, with thousands of Protestants conveniently gathered in Paris, hell broke loose. Whether Catherine personally ordered the massacre or was just complicit in the decision is still debated (she gets blamed for it in many accounts), but the result was a bloodbath of epic proportions. Thousands of Huguenots were killed in Paris and beyond. The streets literally ran red — think of the *Red Wedding* episode from *Game of Thrones*, multiplied by ten and with way fewer survivors. So much for the power of love to bring peace; in this case, a marriage intended to end a war became the pretext for a horrific act of vengeance. Marguerite de Valois, the bride, later wrote that on her wedding night she had to step over the corpses of butchered guests to go see her new husband. (Talk about wedding drama — bridezillas have nothing on 16th-century royals.)

For Catherine, it was a PR disaster of immortally bad reputation. She went from cunning queen to "the evil Italian mother-in-law who massacres houseguests" in the public imagination. It's safe to say *this* wasn't the outcome she wanted from commodifying her daughter's hand in marriage. Yet, from Catherine's cold-eyed perspective, the Huguenots *were* plotting rebellions and the wedding *was* a moment of vulnerability for them, so she seized it. Dark, yes. A distortion of "using love as a weapon"? Absolutely — the wedding was the bait, and murder was the outcome. As a satirical aside, one might say: Catherine wanted her daughter's marriage to *kill the hatred*, but instead it just killed a lot of people. When love becomes a weapon, it can blow up in your face – literally, in this case, with arquebus shots and gruesome mayhem.

Marriages aside, Catherine had other arrows in her quiver. Let's talk about her "Flying Squadron" — which is not a Quidditch team, but rather a notorious cohort of 80 hand-picked young women reputed to be Catherine's elite femme fatale force. These ladies were the *Charlie's Angels* of the 16th century, if Charlie were a steely queen mother in widow's weeds. They earned their nickname from a ballet Catherine hosted where her ladies danced so gracefully they seemed to fly. But the *military* connotation of "squadron" was apt: Catherine deployed these women as beautiful weapons at court. Their mission? Seduce and spy. They would cozy up to powerful men – noblemen, ambassadors, even rebellious princes – glean information, and, when useful, influence these men's actions *in Catherine's favor*. It was honeypot espionage long before James Bond ever ordered a martini. For instance, when Catherine caught wind that her youngest son (the Duke of Alençon) and her son-in-law (Henry of Navarre, yes the same one from the bloody wedding) were conspiring against her around 1577, she unleashed one of her top agents, Charlotte de Sauve.

Charlotte proceeded to seduce *both* men simultaneously, turning them into jealous rivals for her affection and effectively torpedoing their plot. Marguerite de Valois (Catherine's daughter and Henry of Navarre's wife) bitterly noted that Charlotte "so captivated them that they forgot all else – even their conspiracy". In other words, *Mission Accomplished*. Catherine foiled a dangerous alliance without shedding a drop of blood; all it took was a skilled coquette who could play two smitten dudes against each other. A contemporary satirist quipped that Catherine was lucky to have such a "stable of whores" at her command (an insult which tells you how this tactic was viewed by the more puritanical crowd). Insult or not, Catherine probably smirked at that: better to have a stable of "ladies" fighting for you than an army of mercenaries, especially when you're a woman in a man's world and open warfare isn't an option.

The Flying Squadron's exploits became the scandalous talk of Europe. Pamphlets and gossip rags (well, the 16th-century version of them) accused Catherine of throwing debauched parties where her ladies would serve guests in half-dressed costumes, or worse. One famous tale (likely exaggerated) describes a banquet where the squadron appeared topless, painted gold from the waist up, mingling with stunned male guests as living decor – and also as very distracting intelligence-gatherers. True or not, these stories titillated and horrified in equal measure. They cemented Catherine's image as a sinister queen orchestrating a web of seduction. Modern historians debate how real the Flying Squadron really was – some say Catherine's ladies were chosen more for wit and loyalty than for looks and didn't literally sleep with half the court. But Catherine's legend had taken on a life of its own. She was blamed for everything: poisoning rivals with tainted gloves or books (yep, rumor said she had a poison book that would kill you if you touched it), practicing dark sorcery (Nostradamus was one of her astrologers, so that added to her mystical rep), and generally being the shadowy *éminence grise* behind every French political twist for 30 years. Was some of this deserved? Sure. Catherine was indeed ruthless and cunning. When you've lived through being a despised foreign teenager, a sidelined wife, then had to watch your husband die and your sons struggle to hold a kingdom together, you either toughen up or perish. Catherine toughened up *big time.*

And unlike Wu Zetian or the women of the Ottoman harem, Catherine had no official position or harem infrastructure to work with (once her husband died, she was just "the queen mother" – a widow with prestige but theoretically no executive power). She had to innovate, and boy, did she. She effectively ran the French government from backstage, juggling feuding factions (sometimes literally inviting Catholic and Protestant leaders to dinner and then mediating like a marriage counselor) and occasionally deciding a good old-fashioned murder was the way to go. (She almost certainly had a hand in the Duke of Guise's assassination in 1588, for instance, when he threatened her son Henry III's reign.)

Yet, Catherine also has a side that's almost endearing in its dark humor: for example, faced with a shortage of funds and too many feckless nobles, she started a silk-worm farming industry at court to boost the economy (imagine her giving ladies mulberry leaves to feed caterpillars – it's weirdly wholesome). Or when her son Henry III liked to parade around in extravagant costumes, Catherine sighed but footed the bill (she herself popularized black as high fashion – she wore it in perpetual mourning, but made it *chic*). She was a patron of the arts, introduced pasta, perfumes, and ballet to the French court, and threw incredible pageants. In one instance, she engineered a 3-day extravaganza on the canals of the palace at Fontainebleau, featuring boats shaped like whales and dragons, all to impress the Polish envoys into accepting her son Henry as King of Poland. (It worked; they crowned him – though he later ditched Poland to be King of France. Still, A+ for effort, Catherine.)

Through all this, Catherine de' Medici's use of romantic and sexual relationships as tools stands out. Whether marrying off her kids, manipulating amorous liaisons among courtiers, or simply leveraging the fact that men in power often have blind spots where a pretty face is concerned, she played that card deftly. She commodified love – not because she was born a cynic, but because in her world, affection and alliance were commodities *to begin with*. Women like her had to use *every* tool available to survive and thrive. Love, or the appearance of it, was just another tool. Did she love her children? Almost certainly – she fought viciously to secure their legacies. Did she love her husband Henry II? Hard to say; he ignored her for years, yet when he died, she guarded his legacy ferociously (and yes, she finally banished Diane de Poitiers from court after Henry's death – one imagines that was a satisfying palace eviction). Catherine understood power, and if that meant packaging her daughters' hands in marriage deals or turning a blind eye while her ladies entrapped a potential rebel, so be it. Morality took a backseat to raison d'état (the national interest, which, conveniently, often aligned with Catherine's family interest).

Now, let's not paint Catherine as a pure puppet-master and everyone else as puppets. Plenty of her "weapons" had minds of their own (her daughter Margot, for one, who famously did *not* want to be the sacrificial bride to Navarre, ended up having her own wild life including love affairs and a literary career). But Catherine's influence was such that she is remembered as the grand orchestrator, the spider in the center of France's web. In pop culture, she's been portrayed as everything from an outright villain (Dumas's novel *La Reine Margot* has her as a near-poisonous caricature) to a complex antihero (the recent TV series *The Serpent Queen* gives a more cheeky, sympathetic take). If Wu Zetian was like a deadly Queen of Hearts and the Ottoman harem was a whole team of Queen bees, Catherine de' Medici was the Queen Mother who said, "I'll see your patriarchy and raise you a matriarchy from the shadows."

Her story, with its black comedy of errors (the attempted wedding peace treaty that ends in apocalypse) and its salacious espionage episodes, underscores the theme in a witty-yet-pointed way. Catherine essentially turned France into her chessboard, and while she played, *love was her knight, marriage her rook, and sex appeal absolutely her bishop.* (We'll leave the pawns to the poor people who just tried to stay alive through all this.)

So, what's the final tally on Catherine? She kept the Valois dynasty hanging on a bit longer, but all three of her sons died without surviving male issue, and the throne passed to Henry of Navarre – that same Huguenot husband of her daughter, who became Henry IV, first of the Bourbon kings. Ironically, one could joke that after all Catherine's maneuvering, the crown went to her son-in-law whom she once attempted to murder with a honeytrap. History has a wicked sense of humor. Catherine died in 1589, just months before her last son was assassinated; she never saw the ultimate failure of her dynastic dreams. Perhaps it's just as well – it might have killed her, if she weren't already dead.

What she did leave behind was a legacy of statecraft through softer means. No, not soft like easy – soft like in contrast to armies and open decrees. She was the ultimate example that when women weren't allowed to use swords or scepters openly, they would use marriages and masquerades instead. And she did it all with a kind of dark grace that can only be fully appreciated with a slightly twisted sense of humor (which, as you can tell, we've indulged here).

Conclusion: Love's Poisoned Chalice

From Wu Zetian's blood-soaked boudoir maneuvers to the Ottoman harem's cloak-and-dagger concubinage, and on to Catherine de' Medici's marriage treaties and seductive spy ring, we've toured a gallery of history's power players who turned *amour* into ammunition. What do these stories have in common, besides enough plot twists to fuel a hundred Netflix series? In each case, romantic and sexual relationships were weaponized as tools of influence, status, and control. And notably, it was often women — constrained by intensely patriarchal systems — who became the grandmasters of this game, out of necessity and genius, turning the very constraints imposed on them into avenues of power.

There's a satirical saying: *"All's fair in love and war."* Our three stories show what happens when love is war, when hearts and minds are battlefields for ambition. It's both grim and darkly funny. On one hand, you have to admire the sheer audacity and skill of these women. Wu Zetian basically said, *"If I can't be emperor because I'm a woman, watch me prove you wrong,"* and she did — leaving a trail of stunned (and headless) skeptics behind. The women of the Ottoman harem operated in a system that treated them as possessions, so they flipped the script to make their possessor – the Sultan – dependent on them, using the only channels open to them: seduction, childbearing, and intrigue. Catherine de' Medici, a foreigner and a female in a venomous French court, realized that daggers in the dark could be effectively replaced with a well-arranged marriage or a well-timed flirtation. Each of them survived and thrived by mastering the art of commodified love.

But there's a sharp edge to this sword (or perhaps a hidden dagger in this corset). When love becomes a means to an end, it tends to get warped. Affection turns into manipulation; marriage becomes a transaction; passion is feigned as a ploy. The people involved — whether it's the besotted emperors, the jealous concubines, or the pawned-off daughters — often end up emotionally bruised or physically dead. *Love-as-weapon* is indiscriminate: it wounds the target, the wielder, and sometimes the whole realm.

The moral isn't a finger-wagging "shame on these schemers" — rather, it's an observation about the system that made scheming the best option. In a world that denied women conventional power, these women found power unconventionally, but it came at a cost. Trust was scarce, genuine love even scarcer. (One wonders, did Wu Zetian ever sleep soundly next to Emperor Gaozong, or was one eye always open? Did Hurrem Sultan ever regret that her love led Suleiman to kill his own son? Did Catherine de' Medici, who married for alliance and married off her kids the same way, ever wish things could have been more…simple? We can't know, but it's easy to imagine these complexities weighed on them in lonely moments.)

For us modern folks, there's both inspiration and caution in these tales. The inspiration: intelligence, wit, and resilience can carve a path where none is given. These women were handed lemons and made lethal lemonade, flavoring it with a dash of satire (in our retelling, at least). The caution: when relationships turn purely transactional — when love is stripped of its humanity and worn like a mask — everyone loses something. Empires might be won, but peace of mind is forfeited. And occasionally, a lot of heads roll.

On a lighter note, we can appreciate the almost absurd theatricality of it all from our safe historical distance. These stories, though deadly serious in their outcomes, have an element of *theater of the absurd*. There's a reason they continue to captivate us in books, opera, TV dramas. Who doesn't enjoy a good tale of "lover by day, schemer by night" with a side of gallows humor? It's the contrast between the intimate and the ruthless that fascinates — the whispered sweet nothing that might seal someone's doom by morning.

In the end, the grand shared theme here is ambition harnessing intimacy. Love, in its genuine form, is supposed to be selfless, vulnerable, sincere. But in these courts and palaces, love was weaponized — aimed like an arrow at political targets. When love becomes *power*, it ceases to be *love* in the heartfelt sense. It becomes a means, not an end. And that, dear reader, is the dangerous transformation at the heart of our chapter.

So, the moral? Perhaps it's a tongue-in-cheek reminder: *Handle hearts with care — they're volatile when used as grenades.* When someone says "I give you my heart," make sure they're not handing you a ticking time bomb. History has shown that when love is a weapon, nobody is safe — not even the one who wields it. Wu Zetian died with no inscription on her tomb, her legacy contested. The Ottoman harem ladies often saw their sons slain the moment those sons took power (fratricide is a hell of a punishment for winning). Catherine de' Medici safeguarded her family only to see a new dynasty take over anyway, her name forever linked with the massacre that stained her reputation.

And yet, in all this tragedy, there's a final bit of satirical wisdom to extract. These women's stories, exaggerated by myth and male historians in parts, underscore that patriarchy's worst nightmare is a woman who knows her worth and weaponizes the very things meant to subdue her. It's almost comedic justice. The men in these tales set up the rules thinking love would keep women occupied and out of power; instead, love (or its semblance) became the vector of their undoing. There's dark humor in that reversal, isn't there? As if the universe enjoys a bit of irony.

So next time you hear a romantic cliché or see a love story with a happy ending, give a little nod to our trio of historical schemers. They certainly didn't get Disney endings, but they reveal a truth often glossed over: in the great game of power, the heart can be as mighty as the sword — and twice as treacherous. When love is a weapon, *vive la guerre!* ... but also, *mon Dieu*, watch your back.

Chapter 11

Lessons from the Crown – Interpreting Love, Power, and Legacy

Royal romances have always played out on a grand stage – complete with love, duty, and scandal. Think of Cleopatra's love affairs with Julius Caesar and Mark Antony, affairs that were as much political gambits as Hollywood-level drama. Or Shah Jahan, the besotted Mughal emperor who turned his grief into stone: he commissioned the Taj Mahal in 1631 "to house the tomb of his beloved wife, Mumtaz Mahal". Across time and continent – from Henry VIII's six wives to Catherine the Great's lovers, Princess Margaret's secret divorcee romance to Grace Kelly's fairy-tale wedding – patterns emerge. Love often clashes with crown and country, transforming empires and hearts alike. These royal stories may feel larger than life, but in truth they are gilded versions of our own passions and politics. And, as we'll see, honest love still reigns supreme.

Love and Duty: The Royal Tug-of-War

Modern readers might picture thrones and tuxedos, but at any court in history the struggle between personal desire and dynastic duty is eternal. A throne is more than a chair – it's a chair plus a spreadsheet of alliances, and the boss (king or queen) often has to choose between their heart and their heads of state. Cleopatra VII, for example, famously "fell in love affairs that were ... power struggles". Her alliances with Julius Caesar and Mark Antony were as politically charged as any modern merger, and ultimately shaped the fate of Rome and Egypt. Likewise, Edward VIII put love above crown: after only 11 months as king he "abdicated in order to marry Wallis Simpson", a divorcee who the government could not accept. The only British monarch ever to resign the throne, Edward proved that even palaces can't prevent a love-addled heart from jumping ship. Princess Margaret, Elizabeth II's younger sister, lived a similar story of conflict. In the 1950s, Margaret was "forced to choose between royal duty and the man she wants to marry, divorced royal equerry Peter Townsend". Her Catholic background and the Church's rules made marrying a divorced man impossible – despite the real love between them – and Margaret quietly surrendered to duty.

Even when love does not lead to abdication, it often forces a sort of political triage. Henry VIII, the ultimate example of crown-over-comfort, famously chased a male heir above all; he is "largely remembered for having six wives". The kids-to-king priority meant divorce, execution, and fallout. Henry's desperate emotional commerce (often colorfully summarized as *divorced, beheaded, died...*) illustrates the nightmare side of love under a crown. Catherine of Aragon might have escaped execution, but Henry still sought an annulment for the same reason that got Anne Boleyn beheaded: dynastic necessity. At heart, many royals play out a kind of wild tug-of-war between following their heart and securing their heirs. In far-flung courts and different centuries, from England to

India, the message is the same: Hearts may ache, but thrones still demand spin.

Dynastic Alliances – Corporate Mergers in Tiaras

Royal marriages of state were basically the ancient equivalent of hostile takeovers. If you think corporate mergers can get complicated, try padding your wedding guest list with dukes, popes, and Holy Roman Emperors. Dynastic weddings often united kingdoms the way two companies consolidate stocks – and love often took a backseat. When Ferdinand of Aragon married Isabella of Castile on October 19, 1469, it "beg[an] a cooperative reign that would unite all the dominions of Spain". In practical terms, this marriage was the literal merger that formed modern Spain (and set the stage for Columbus). As one historian notes, Isabella's 1469 marriage to Ferdinand "created the basis of the de facto unification of Spain". In other words, it was a royal *power couple* in the most literal sense, hard-wiring new empires via contract rather than candlelit confessionals.

Think of it this way: the royal matrimonial agenda often read like the minutes of a board meeting. Marrying off princesses and princes could secure borders, subdue rivals, and even establish international trade – all while keeping things in the family. (Yes, the family reunions were awkward.) A clever monarch knew that love was optional at best. Henry VIII's marriage to Catherine of Aragon, himself a Spanish prince, initially secured a Spanish alliance – and only became personal when he decided he needed a Henry VIII, not a daughter. When Courtiers saw angle on a throne, they brokered merger deals marked down in marriage contracts. A modern analogy might be "Queen Mary & Co." IPOs or "Royal Holdings" share swaps.

Royal hats off to those matchmakers: dynastic marriages created empires and were legally binding as any corporate merger agreement.

Of course, as in any corporate takeover, divorces and hostile exits happened too. Elizabeth I's suitors famously found she would rather run an empire solo than merge. But Henry VIII showed how messy it could get: two wives down and he still didn't get what he wanted. Meanwhile in Asia, Empress Wu Zetian used marriage (and more violent tactics) to climb the ladder. She first won over Emperor Gaozong (her stepson) and sidelined his official wife. Legend (and history books) say Wu Zetian literally bumped off a baby to depose her rival and become empress herself. In corporate terms: she was the ultimate hostile takeover. Within a year, she ousted Empress Wang from the throne to become Wu Hou, later Emperor Zetian. It was nepotism, intrigue and even alleged infanticide all wrapped into one historical IPO. In short, royal marriages could create and destroy dynasties like financial fictions – only the logos were crowns and the dividends were heirs.

Drama and Scandal: Palace Reality TV

Strike up the band – palace walls have seen more drama than a season of *Game of Thrones*. If today's tabloids love star divorces and cheating scandals, just rewind a few centuries and swap paparazzi for palace servants. Edward VIII and Wallis Simpson were the eighteenth-century *royal TMZ*: when Edward fell "deeply in love" with Wallis, Britain's establishment threw a hissy fit. The result? He abdicated. Princess Diana might have broken royal protocol by wearing pants at a polo match, but Edward dropped the crown for a divorcee – a scandal of Shakespearean proportions. And that Windsor scandal was only the beginning. King James I of England (also James VI of Scotland) had favorites whose influence caused endless palace gossip. King James "initially rose to prominence because the homosexual James found him [the Duke of Buckingham] physically and emotionally appealing," fueling an infamous liaison. In modern terms, Buckingham was like a favored celebrity BFF whose every appearance made headlines and courtiers nervous. James's preferences scandalized yet enthralled his court; Catherine the Great's lovers were whispered about in Catherine the Great's Russia as if it were a reality spin-off (one estimate says she had a string of powerful favorites, perhaps none more famed than Grigory Potemkin).

Even catastrophes got tabloid treatment. Shah Jahan's beloved Mumtaz Mahal died in childbirth, and the emperor's grief wasn't private – he hired 20,000 artisans to literally write his love on earth. Though the Taj Mahal stands silent, contemporaries likened it to a "teardrop on the cheek of time." It's like if a CEO built the world's most elaborate memorial after a divorce – only with more marble. On the flip side, royals have been divorced and exiled by their own headlines. Princess Margaret's heartbreak was national news: Britain watched her drama unfold (and The Crown re-enacted it) as she chose duty over Townsend. Compared to any reality show, these narratives had everything: secret romances, jealous rivals, and end-of-season cliffhangers. History's palace intrigues were *Peak TV* – minus the commercials.

Cross-Cultural Romances and Unexpected Alliances

In our globalized world, international relationships seem normal. But centuries ago, cross-culture royal romances were exotic epics. Imagine hearing that an American actress married a prince in Monaco – Grace Kelly did just that, in what was "a real-life fairytale" on April 19, 1956. Grace Kelly traded Hollywood for a tiara, proving even a small kingdom could bridge a cultural divide. Or consider Queen Noor of Jordan, born Lisa Halaby in Washington D.C. – she became King Hussein's fourth wife in 1978. An American princess by choice, Noor's marriage wasn't just an exotic romance but a genuine love match that crossed continents. (Her very title, Noor "Al Hussein," means light, symbolizing how far love can reach.)

These modern fairy tales echo older traditions. Catherine the Great herself was German-born Sophie, yet she outmaneuvered Russian courtiers to become Empress. And centuries earlier, Isabella of Castile (a Castilian Spanish princess) wedded Ferdinand of Aragon (from a different realm) – their union created Spain's Golden Age. Cross-cultural marriages often turned kingdoms into cosmopolitan powers. They also stirred public fascination; headlines in their day spoke of exotic brides and brokers of peace more than gossip columnists did. The lesson? Love doesn't respect borders. Whether by handbag from Hollywood to Monte Carlo or by treaty in Renaissance Spain, royal hearts often found one another across the divides of race, nation, and tradition. And when they did, the resulting cultures were richer for it.

Secrets, Same-Sex Affections, and Hidden Passions

Not every royal affair was printed on gilded invitation cards. Many romances were whispered secrets in gilded halls – some even same-sex romances shrouded in palace mystery. King James I of England is a prime example. Historian Paul Hunneyball notes that James (VI/I) "initially rose to prominence because the homosexual James found [Buckingham] physically and emotionally appealing," which sustained their decade-long affair. These passionate preferences certainly scandalized many, yet James's case shows that even absolute monarchs had private lives full of the very same desires we see today. (Remember, this was the king who funded the Bible translation, so talk about a double life!) In China, Empress Wu Zetian kept her relationships quiet at first, but legend has it she caught Emperor Gaozong's eye while he was still married. With destiny in mind, she deftly schemed to remove his wife and become empress herself. It's rumored she even blamed an infant's death on her rivals to clear her path to the throne. While these may sound like medieval soap-operas, the underlying theme is modern: power often shadows private passion, and where power moves, love often lurks behind the scenes.

Across cultures, royals who loved unconventionally had to be creative. Some hid feelings, some paraded lovers in secret, some used marriages as cover. What unites them is the authenticity of their emotion. Even a queen in a foreign court felt her Spanish princess sister's drama (Queen Isabella's sister Joanna went mad for love). When we look at the archives, these hidden stories are not so different from modern ones – affairs, heartbreaks, and secret identities. History shows: even emperors had hearts that skipped beats off the record.

Enduring Transformation and Legacy

Time and again, royal love and loss have led to profound change. When Mumtaz Mahal died, Shah Jahan was "inconsolable" and turned grief into "the ultimate testament of his love" – the Taj Mahal. A mausoleum that took decades and an empire's treasury to complete, it stands today as a symbol of how love can inspire lasting beauty. That's transformation of pain into legacy. Catherine the Great was in love and in power simultaneously: aided by lover Grigory Orlov, she usurped her husband's throne just six months after he took power. Her coup wasn't romantic in the usual sense, but it transformed Russia – and showed how a royal romance can be seething with ambition.

Other royals evolved through love and loss, even if quietly. Princess Margaret, denied the match she wanted, instead poured herself into public service (and off-camera affairs) – in a way, surviving emotionally by reinventing herself beyond court gossip. Edward VIII found that abdication and exile forced him to create a new life; Grace Kelly transformed from movie star to governess of Monaco, shaping the tiny principality's future (her children and even her granddaughter Charlotte Casiraghi still link Monaco to Hollywood today). Across these chapters, one sees transformation as a theme: authentic love often required reinvention, whether building cathedrals of marble (Taj), founding new dynasties (Wu Zetian's Zhou Dynasty), or quietly ensuring heirs (Ferdinand and Isabella's children included European monarchs for generations).

In every case, honesty mattered. The royals who tried to fake, cheat, or forcibly suppress love often left wreckage. Those who acknowledged it – for better or worse – left art, stories, and sometimes a better world. Our last takeaway: the heart's truth, even in royalty, is the longest-lasting statute of all.

Reflections and Recurring Themes

- Love vs. Duty: Royals often faced "a clash of loyalty" between personal passion and state responsibility. From Cleopatra to Catherine of Aragon, history shows that choosing duty could save an empire, while choosing love could cost a crown.

- Marriage as Alliance: Many royal marriages were effectively political mergers. These union of crowns united peoples like corporate takeovers, often "unifying kingdoms" at the expense of true romance. When love did creep into these deals, it either cemented a realm (as with Ferdinand & Isabella) or sparked crisis (as with Henry VIII).

- Scandal & Secrecy: Palace walls harbored far more intrigue than most realize. Affairs – whether Edward VIII's or King James's – could topple governments or reshape dynasties. Love was often the secret sauce behind coups and abdications. When tabloids didn't exist, whispering courtiers filled the gap, but the outcome was the same: emotions unearthed, reputations upended.

- Cross-Cultural Romance: Monarchs sometimes fell for foreigners, blurring borders of love. Grace Kelly's 1956 wedding was truly "a real-life fairytale" that brought Hollywood glamour to Monaco. Queen Noor's 1978 marriage to King Hussein united East and West. Such romances remind us that love transcends nationality, making even the most divergent worlds feel a little closer.

- Love's Legacy: Finally, the biggest pattern is legacy. Grief has birthed monuments (the Taj Mahal), abdications have rewritten history (Edward VIII), and clandestine love has quietly influenced policy behind every throne. No matter the century, the stories end the same: honest love endures as the greatest sovereign of all. After all the banquets, battles, and backstabbing, the truest measure of royalty has always been human emotion.

In the end, what do these magnified love stories tell us? That history's grandest stage is hardly different from our own living rooms. The only difference is the costumes – and maybe the crown, a heavy reminder that true love often has to outlast thrones. Royal love stories, in all their wild complexity, turn out to be just very elaborate mirrors: reflections of our own secret longings, betrayals, joys, and griefs – only with more pageantry. Through centuries and cultures, one thing remains constant: when royals loved honestly, that love ruled more enduringly than any king or queen ever could.

Epilogue

The Final Curtain on Crowned Capers

The Absurdity of Crowned Hearts

After this rollicking journey through palace intrigue and romantic misadventures, one thing is clear: royalty never did anything by halves, especially not in love. We've witnessed kings and queens fall headlong into passion and peril, proving that the higher the throne, the harder (and more theatrically) one can fall. From a queen who smuggled herself in a carpet to meet her lover, to a sultan who elevated a harem consort to queen, to emperors who built monuments for a beloved (only to perhaps regret the expense), each tale blurred the line between the absurd and the human. Lust, betrayal, ambition, ego – every scandalous twist was a reminder that behind the tiaras and titles were people just as prone to folly as the rest of us.

Indeed, if power corrupts, love absolutely bedazzles. We saw a Tudor king solve his marital woes by splitting with the Church (and splitting from a few wives' heads, too) – an extreme form of "taking a break." A French queen's innocent flirtation could spark gossip that put Instagram rumors to shame. Time and again, royal romance demanded a strong stomach – for drama, that is – whether in clandestine letters by moonlight or wars ignited over a lover's slight.

The absurdity dazzled and occasionally horrified, yet through it all a warm thread of humanity wove under the velvet and ermine.

Lessons on Royal Love

So, what can we commoners learn from this parade of crowned capers? History doesn't repeat itself, but it does instruct. Here are a few tongue-in-cheek relationship lessons from the royal playbook:

- Don't marry your cousin just to preserve the bloodline. Royal families tried it and family trees got weird. (Bonus: Your future kids – and *jawlines* – will thank you.)

- Communicate before launching a war. Misunderstandings at court once led to real battles. Next time your beloved leaves the toilet seat up, take a deep breath and talk it out – it's cheaper and far less messy than a civil war.

- Beware of mysterious court astrologers. If some robed guru insists the stars oppose your union, get a second opinion. Many a royal could've saved themselves heartache (and *headache*) by relying on honest conversation over horoscopes.

Each outrageous anecdote comes with a wink and a nod. They're playful warnings, sure, but behind each chuckle lies a sincere truth: even the mightiest rulers can get it wrong in love, and we can all learn from their blunders – preferably while laughing from a safe historical distance.

Crowns Off to Love

In the grand saga of human affairs, it turns out love laughs last. After all the betrayals, bedchamber plots, dramatic divorces, and unimaginable scandals, we arrive at this: love remains gloriously, stubbornly human. Kings and queens were never immune to heartbreak or giddy infatuation. In a way, that's comforting. The whims of Cupid spare no one, and amid royal chaos we find a mirror of our own hearts.

So here's a final royal decree: embrace the marvelous insanity of love, but leave the poison and palace coups to the history books. If emperors and empresses kept chasing "happily ever after" – one even trading his crown for it – despite the pitfalls, there's hope for the rest of us. Long live love, in all its unruly glory – may we cherish it, learn from it, and handle it with a bit more grace than those poor royals did. And to you, dear reader, who braved this carnival of kings and consorts: go forth and write your own story – preferably with far fewer beheadings. Cheers to love – the one crown jewel we all share.

www.ingramcontent.com/pod-product-compliance
Lightning Source LLC
Chambersburg PA
CBHW061742120626
46550CB00005B/1858